Wicked
LITCHFIELD
COUNTY

Wicked
Litchfield
County

•••

Peter C. Vermilyea

THE
History
PRESS

Published by The History Press
Charleston, SC
www.historypress.net

First published 2016

Manufactured in the United States

ISBN 978.1.46711.969.6

Library of Congress Control Number: 2016932068

For my mother and father, wicked good parents

CONTENTS

ACKNOWLEDGEMENTS

The idea for this book originated with a walking tour my wife and I participated in while visiting Newport, Rhode Island. It introduced us to the "rogues and scoundrels" who lived among the Gilded Age splendor of that city. I was intrigued by the idea of whether this approach could be utilized for Litchfield County. For the idea behind *Wicked Litchfield County*, I owe a special thanks to our guide, Lew Keene. And for their willingness to let me explore these stories and their unflinching support, a big thank-you is owed to Tabitha Dulla and Karmen Cook of The History Press.

As with *Hidden History of Litchfield County*, this book would not have been possible without the staff of the Litchfield Historical Society. Cathy Fields and Liz O'Grady provided me with opportunities to try out this material with audiences. Alex DuBois provided assistance with artifacts and paintings. And Linda Hocking again went above and beyond in securing images and passing along sources and tips. I'd also be remiss if I didn't thank my fellow board members for their support of my work.

Also in Litchfield, the staff of the Oliver Wolcott Library, especially Cameron Bove and Audra MacLaren, is always tremendously helpful. Jim Strub and Ed O'Connell provide excellent advice and encouragement, and Mike Main patiently listened to ideas for this book as we ran the roads and trails of Litchfield. Emily McAdam, my son's history teacher, provided the insights into the origin of the name of Litchfield.

My friend and colleague Warren Prindle again provided invaluable assistance with the book's images and was always willing to listen to ideas.

Acknowledgements

A special thank-you to my students at Housatonic Valley Regional High School, who teach me new things every day. Susan Shephard graciously shared her research on counterfeiters, Rufus de Rham provided a key source and Lawrence Donohue gave a lead on a photo. My former students Oliver Martinez, Ed Martinez and Deborah Chabrian provided important assistance with the Molly Fisher Rock. Will Siss provided insight into Prohibition in Connecticut. I have taken great pleasure over the years talking history with Mike DeMazza, Howard Lewis, Jared Peatman and Dennis Perreault.

The staffs of the New Milford Public Library and Woodbury Public Library provided assistance, and Marge Smith of the Kent Historical Society consistently provides interesting ideas. Thanks also to Peg Giles of DeMars Images and Bill Ahrens of the Winchester Historical Society for their assistance, as well as Sierra Dixon of the Connecticut Historical Society and Jackie Penny of the American Antiquarian Society. I owe a debt of gratitude to all the historical societies, libraries, community centers and bookstores that hosted me to discuss *Hidden History*. They were, without exception, sources of encouragement and ideas.

Last but certainly not least is my family. My mother-in-law, Sandy Hovland, is a peerless copy editor, and my father-in-law, Dennis Hovland, is a great promoter of my work. This book is dedicated to my parents, Pete and Kathy Vermilyea, who with my sister, Megan, were—and remain—incredibly indulgent and patient with my interest in history. My wife, Jill, and sons, Ben and Luke, have climbed over boulders, across ice fields and through thickets of prickers in tracking down obscure historical sites. They've offered insights, taken pictures, commented on text and listened patiently to even my really bad ideas. They are my rock, and I owe them thanks for so much more than their help with this book.

INTRODUCTION

$\mathcal{M}$y morning drive to work is along Route 63 North, from Litchfield to Falls Village. It's an ideal commute, not too far, but long enough to mentally prepare for the day. There is never a worry about traffic, and there is always the spectacular view from Roberts Hill. When I tell people about this ride, they invariably respond, "God's country!"

And, historically speaking, God's country is an appropriate term. In my earlier book, *Hidden History of Litchfield County*, I wrote that "there were no presidents born in Litchfield County, nor any famous battles fought within its borders. The county, however, has made an indelible mark on the nation's religious history." This was the home to influential religious leaders, from Joseph Bellamy, the eighteenth-century "Pope of Litchfield County," and Lyman Beecher to the candidate for sainthood, Father Michael McGivney. And the religious zeal unleashed by these prominent theologians resulted in the county being a hotbed for moral reform.

But the notion of God's country also conjures up images of land untouched by man, of an untamed wilderness. And this was certainly what Litchfield County represented to its earliest settlers. Outside of Woodbury, most of the county's towns were settled seven to eight decades after much of the rest of the state. To the earliest settlers, the wilderness represented isolation and danger. This is why nearly all of the county's towns, in their earliest days, offered bounties for wolves, rattlesnakes and mountain lions. It seems clear in looking back on the past that while the county's landscape provided farmlands, streams for mills and the means to run iron furnaces, early settlers feared that evil lurked beneath that landscape's surface.

....

Litchfield draws its name from Litchfield, England, whose name might be derived from the Latin *Letocetum* and the old English *feld*, which came to mean "open country." Any modern-day resident or visitor to Litchfield County, Connecticut, recognizes the inaccuracy of this description of the

Litchfield County residents of the Victorian era were quick to believe they shared their towns with ghosts. *Collection of the Litchfield Historical Society, Litchfield, Connecticut.*

state's northwest corner, which is covered by forests and home to the state's highest terrain. Thus another potential derivation of Litchfield might be more appropriate.

During the reign of the Roman emperor Diocletian, around AD 300, a mass martyrdom of one thousand Christians allegedly took place in the fields of central Britain. The area was named Litchfield, from the word *lich*, meaning dead, or, in some tellings, the undead.

The undead are beyond the scope of this book, which avoids the supernatural in favor of that which is historically documented. But it looks at facets of Litchfield County's history with which those great theological minds would have been uncomfortable, the darker side of human nature.

The county's early residents believed in witches and accused some of their neighbors of sorcery. Later, they believed in ghosts and were fascinated when the reflection of lights in early photos yielded apparent orbs and specters. Some of Litchfield's sons killed their neighbors and for their crimes were hanged on the side of a hill in the county seat. Other residents may not have committed crimes as violent but counterfeited currency with astonishing frequency.

While some of the county's sons were war heroes, others performed less honorably; still other veterans from the Litchfield Hills were the victims of what can be termed wicked behavior or motives. And those ministers, who contributed so much to the region's history, were not always above reproach.

....

This then is, in some ways, a companion to *Hidden History of Litchfield County*. If that book looked to shine a light on the ways residents have commemorated their rich history, this book examines things they hoped their descendants would forget.

1

LITCHFIELD COUNTY'S WITCHES

Theories have abounded for centuries about the meaning of the unusual marks on the boulder on Lane's Hill in Kent. Are they directions to a pirate's treasure? Ancient Celtic symbols? The directions to a supernatural incantation? Regardless of the truth behind their origin, the scratches open a door through which the history of witchcraft in Litchfield County can be viewed.

Witches remain the indelible image of wicked New England. While history and popular culture have traditionally intersected with the story of the Salem witch hunt, historian John Demos—whose *Entertaining Satan* remains a seminal work on witchcraft—has written that this emphasis on Salem leaves us with an "impoverished, not to say distorted, view of a germinal phase in our people's history." New England's witches have a history significantly longer and richer than the events that took place north of Boston in 1692.

Connecticut's earliest residents were particularly fearful of witches because they came from an area of England that was rife with witchcraft prosecution. These early Nutmeggers were also greatly concerned about threats to their new settlements and, as active Puritans, believed that witches were instruments of the devil, used to "corrupt and destroy" their ideal Christian communities, what they deemed a "City on a Hill." For example, in 1693, the Reverend Cotton Mather, a leading Puritan theological leader, wrote of the dangers of witches, who constituted "a horrible plot against the country…The wretches have proceeded to concert and consult the methods of rooting out the Christian religion from this country."

The Wonders of the Invisible World :

Being an Account of the

T R Y A L S

OF

Several Witches,

Lately Excuted in

NEW-ENGLAND:

And of several remarkable Curiosities therein Occurring.

Together with,

I. Observations upon the Nature, the Number, and the Operations of the Devils.

II. A short Narrative of a late outrage committed by a knot of Witches in *Swede-Land*, very much resembling, and so far explaining, that under which *New-England* has laboured.

III. Some Councels directing a due Improvement of the Terrible things lately done by the unusual and amazing Range of *Evil-Spirits* in *New-England*.

IV. A brief Discourse upon those *Temptations* which are the more ordinary Devices of Satan.

By *COTTON MATHER.*

Published by the Special Command of his EXCELLENCY the Govencur of the Province of the *Massachusetts-Bay* in *New-England.*

Printed first, at *Boston* in *New-England* ; and Reprinted at *London*, for *John Dunton*, at the *Raven* in the *Poultry*. 1693.

The frontispiece from Cotton Mather's 1693 exposition of witches. Mather viewed witchcraft as Satan's attempt to overthrow the Puritan "City on a Hill." *Library of Congress.*

The usual means of dealing with witches was to identify them and attempt—through ministerial or medical means—to reform them. When this failed, as it almost always did, witches were brought to trial, and then the convicted witch was used to identify other witches. Following this, witches would be given an opportunity to repent before their execution. From the colony's earliest days, magistrates were empowered to handle defense, probate and justice for Connecticut's towns. They also took an active role in prosecuting witches. This prosecution, however, was grounded in scripture; in fact, laws against witchcraft were often referred to as Mosaic laws because they were drawn from the Old Testament. Leviticus 20:28, for example, states, "A man also or woman that hath a familiar spirit, or that is a wizard, shall surely be put to death: they shall stone them with stones: their blood *shall be* upon them." And these magistrates made sure there was no doubt that witchcraft was a crime against religion, as a typical indictment declared of the accused, "Not having the fear of God before your eyes, you have entertained familiarity with Satan the great enemy of God and mankind and, by his help, have done works against the course of nature."

Incidents of witchcraft were often very closely tied to feelings within a community that they had wandered from God's desired path. This frequently meant that the town residents had neglected their religious obligations, turned excessively to alcohol, repeatedly disturbed the peace or engaged in "nightwalking" (which usually referred to theft or prostitution). Such actions, it was feared, allowed an opening for the devil to inhabit their community. Identifying and punishing these witches represented the triumph of God and the values of the Puritan community.

While the simple act of being a witch was technically a crime, in reality, another person needed to suffer some sort of injury for the expense and effort of witchcraft prosecution to be justified. Still, 234 residents of colonial New England were accused of witchcraft, 36 of whom were ultimately executed. This represents a higher rate of "success" in witch hunting than in England— testimony, perhaps, to the religious fervor that was present in the colonies.

John Demos has found that the typical accused witch was a middle-aged woman of English Puritan stock. She was married but had either no children or a number significantly fewer than the eight to nine children the average colonial New England mother had. Accused witches were frequently from a lower class, were often in conflict with other family members and had likely been accused of some other crime (usually involving some sort of aggressive or offensive speech). Importantly, these women were also often practitioners of "doctoring" or alternative medicine.

Twenty-first-century Americans tend to think of their colonial ancestors as rugged individualists, and while it certainly took a great deal of courage to carve an existence out of the New England wilderness, they also struggled with fears and insecurities. Demos has written that these colonists were "persistently vulnerable in their core sense of self," and these uncertainties "plagued their ability to grow and endure as free-standing individuals." In other words, when things went wrong in their communities, colonial New Englanders were liable to fear the worst, and for a fervently religious population, that meant the supernatural.

....

Connecticut's witch hunts, with their subsequent executions, took place within a relatively small window of time: 1647 to 1663. (It is interesting to note that Connecticut's last execution of a witch took place nearly thirty years before the Salem Witch Trials.) While this predates the founding of all Litchfield County towns, legends of witches dot the region's history.

By the eighteenth century, witches were no longer seen as being deadly. Rather, they were eccentrics, and their actions were increasingly in the realm of inflicting nuisances (breads that wouldn't rise, butter that wouldn't churn), inducing prurient nightmares or making simple mischief, such as causing others embarrassment or confusion. While execution and all other forms of legal punishment for witchcraft were taken off the books in Connecticut in 1750, the social ostracism practiced against eighteenth-century witches meant that they often suffered more than their alleged victims.

Litchfield County's late founding meant that conditions were rife for residents to accuse their neighbors of being witches long after it had fallen out of fashion in the rest of Connecticut. The region's isolation, which led to the joke, "Yes, go to Cornwall and you will have no need of a jail, for whoever gets in can never get out again," certainly caused residents to fear the unknown of the dark woods. Also, the county was known as a hotbed for religious zeal, with the Congregational Church playing a central role not only in theological matters but also in political and cultural affairs. Such religious fervor caused the particularly pious to see Satan's hand in their neighbors' decisions to eschew the church.

It is worth noting that there were very real things for these people to be afraid of, which in their ferocity, seemed to have come from a supernatural source. These were diseases, which ravaged the county in its early years. Sharon, founded in 1739, began with great promise and prosperity, but calamity struck in May 1742. An illness, described by an early county history as a "wasting sickness," overwhelmed the town so dramatically that it needed to apply to the colonial assembly for relief from its debts, bonds and even its obligations to its minister. That minister, the Reverend Peter Pratt, wrote the appeal to the assembly:

> *In May last it pleased the Almighty to send a nervous fever among us, which continued eleven months, in which time more than one hundred, and twenty persons were long confined with it, some have lain more than one hundred days, some eighty, many sixty, and few have been capable of business in forty days after they were seized with the distemper. By reason of which, many were unable to plow for wheat in the year past, many who had plowed were unable to sow, and some who had sowed unable to secure it by fence, and much wheat that was ripe, rotted on the ground…Twenty are dead, many widows and fatherless children are left among us, not a man but that has sustained loss—many who were more than level with the world are impoverished…Many men are obliged to leave their business at home, and go twenty miles to labor for bread and corn.*

The situation in Sharon was deemed so severe that the assembly granted the town a three-year grace period for paying its debts.

A similar event took place in Bethlehem in 1760 when the "Great Sickness" struck the town in November. Thirty-four died after displaying symptoms first of the common cold and then of malignant pleurisy. Dr. Zephaniah Hull; his wife, Hannah; two of their children; and a young man who was boarding with the family all succumbed to the illness, Hull and his wife being buried in the same grave. Deacon Samuel Strong, passing by the Hulls' house while the family lay ill, "raised a flock of eleven quail, which flew over the house and dropped in the garden. Immediately after three rose and flew into the bushes, but the other eight were picked up dead, and in one hour after became putrid and were buried." Death was so rampant in the small town that the air itself was proclaimed by doctors to have been "different from the air in towns and parishes round about it." In a society that knew nothing about germ theory, what besides the hand of Satan could be responsible for such apocalypses?

•••••••••••••••••••••

This, then, was the environment in which Litchfield County's witch stories emerged. While there are certainly others, two of these stories stand out both for their corroboration (not of supernatural activity, but of concern raised by neighbors) and their impact on the county's history. Much can be learned about attitudes toward witches (and women in general, for that matter) by the shared name of Moll Cramer of Woodbury and Molly Fisher of Kent. "Moll" or "Molly" originated as a euphemism for a prostitute in the early seventeenth century. Its use was later expanded to include women who acted outside the gender expectations held by society. For example, the marital adventures, grifting and outright thievery perpetrated by the protagonist of Daniel Defoe's novel led to her being named Moll Flanders.

Moll Cramer lived on Grassy Hill near Transylvania Brook, the area along the current Woodbury and Roxbury border, in the 1750s. As Moll lived before Roxbury became an entity separate from Woodbury, she is traditionally listed as having inhabited the latter town. She married blacksmith Adam Cramer, who was described as a good "Christian man." The couple had a son, also named Adam. However, according to the *Ancient History of Woodbury*, Adam

Good Hill, on the Woodbury/Roxbury town line, was the reported home of Moll Cramer. *Photo by author.*

Sr. soon realized that if he was "so unlucky as to fall under [Moll's] ire, everything went wrong with him." Legends persist that if Moll desired, no number of nails could keep a shoe on a horse. With the neighbors—his customers—terrified of Moll, Adam felt he had no recourse but to declare that his wife had "familiarity with Satan" and cast her out of their home.

Moll and her son, who was believed to have been bewitched by his mother, removed to a ramshackle wooden structure on Grassy Hill, where they slept on straw and survived by begging from the neighbors, who were too terrified to refuse her supplications. Reports swirled that if Moll's request of pork was denied, a blight would fall upon the farmer's hogs. Nor was it only rejection of Moll's specific appeals that brought retribution; one story relates that Moll visited a neighbor who was churning butter. When after a certain amount of time no cream was offered, Moll left the house. The woman continued to churn into the night and the next morning, but no butter ever appeared. According to a nineteenth-century town history of Woodbury:

> After a long time it occurred to the churner and her husband that Moll had been there the day before, and that she had doubtless bewitched the cream. The good man of the house, determining to burn the witch out of the cream, heated a horse shoe and dropped it into the churn. A few moments after, the process of churning ceased, and the butter was "gathered." If these good people had been a little better acquainted with nature's laws, they would have understood that the heat imparted by the shoe, was just the warmth required to accomplish the purpose, and would not have supposed that any miracle had been performed in burning the witch!

This advice seems easier for an author of the late 1800s, who lived in a society relatively free of the fear of witches that plagued New England a century earlier, to give than for Moll's neighbors in the 1750s.

It was alleged that Moll's mere appearance at the door would cause the wheel of a spinning jenny to fly off. Girls who secretly gathered grapes near Moll's shack thought they had not been seen but upon reaching their home found that their delicious harvest had been rendered inedible. It is interesting to note, however, that children, upon seeing Moll, fled to the schoolhouse, where they were protected by their teacher. As schools in colonial America were, to a certain extent, offshoots of churches, there is in this story an element of the crucifix being used to ward off vampires.

Genealogical records suggest that Adam Sr. may, with Miriam Cleveland, have had a son, Henry, who was born in 1766 and moved to Vermont in the

1780s. Of Moll Cramer and her son, Adam, however, no records exist to say if they remained in Woodbury, if Adam married or had children of his own or when they died.

·····················

A similar, although less well-documented, story played out in Kent. In 1789, Ezra Stiles, the president of Yale College who had a great interest in geology (especially in unusual geological formations and mysterious carvings), traveled to the town to investigate a rock that students had brought to his attention. Stiles wrote:

> Over against Scaticook and about one hundred rods East of the Housatonic River, is an eminence or elevation which is called Cobble Hill. On the top of this stands the rock charged with antique unknown characters. This rock is by itself and not a portion of the Mountains; it is of White Flint; ranges North and South; is from twelve to fourteen feet long; and from eight to ten wide at base and top; and of an uneven surface. On the top I did not perceive any characters; but the sides all around are irregularly charged with unknown characters, made not indeed with the incision of a chisel, yet most certainly with an iron tool, and that by pecks or picking, after the manner of Dighton Rock. The Lacunae or excavations are from a quarter to an inch wide; and from one tenth to two tenths of an inch deep. The engraving did not appear to be recent or new, but very old.

Stiles thus became one of the earliest observers to describe what is known as Molly Fisher's Rock, a glacial erratic that continues to befuddle the curious.

But what of the woman behind the rock? Molly Fisher was born around 1750 and, while reported to have been very beautiful, never married. She was what a twenty-first-century crowd might call a drifter; without a home of her own in the community, she nonetheless unexpectedly appeared to assist with the care of the sick, caring for them, as local historian Clifford Spooner wrote, "with her uncanny skill with herbs, and on their recovery disappear[ed] as suddenly as she had come." Fisher was also legendary for her Robin Hood quality, bringing articles of great value to Kent residents which were later found to have come—willingly or not—from the town's well-to-do.

Alleged engravings on the Molly Fisher Rock in Kent. *Photo by author.*

Where the story of Molly Fisher differs from the story of Moll Cramer is in the attitudes toward the women held by the respective residents of Kent and Woodbury. While the townsfolk of Woodbury lived in fear of Cramer, there appears to have been genuine affection shown to Fisher by the people of Kent. Some thought Molly was a witch; others thought she was mentally ill. Regardless, many took her into their homes, freely offered her food and celebrated her as a member of their community.

Still, the legends remain, and most of them have to do with the rock. Some claim that Molly was seen there chanting and speaking in tongues. The carvings were left by her as supernatural messages. Others maintain that Fisher left the markings as a warning to Native Americans and that similar rocks across the state—in Saybrook, for example—are also messages left by Molly. Perhaps the most persistent story declares that Molly was the secret wife of the famed pirate Captain William Kidd and that the rock denotes the hiding spot of Kidd's lost treasure. A history of the area written in the 1930s alleges that a visitor to Kent went digging for the treasure in the early 1800s and nearly succeeded in making off with it, but the curse of Molly Fisher doomed his effort at the last minute. That Kidd was hanged in 1701, long before any settlers appeared in Kent and half a century before Fisher's approximate date of birth, has done little to quash the legends. In fact, Molly Fisher was even referenced in the television series *Lost*.

....

A similar story was unfolding in Winchester. Up until 1760, only four families had inhabited the town: the Beaches, Motts, Prestons and Filleys. These families necessarily intermarried, so it is not surprising to find Caleb Beach, the first settler of the town, selling his Hall Meadow home to the Filleys, who were his sons-in-law. What may have made it unusual was that Mrs. Filley was suspected by her fellow Winchester residents of being a witch.

The stories are entertaining, if predictable. One night, a passerby was making his way along the corduroy road that traversed a swamp when he heard a young child crying in the woods and then, as one early Winsted historian has written, "shrieks of maniacal laughter." He raced home, tripping over the stumps and stones that marked the early roads of the county. The next morning, he ran into Mrs. Filley, who pointed a skinny finger at him and cackled, "Ha! Ha! Awful skeered last night, wan't ye!"

On the road from Burrville to Winchester stood the Shingle House, known to many as a house of ill repute. A man who had enjoyed an evening there was walking back to Winchester when he saw a black dog lying in the road. Nearing the dog, he kicked it, but his foot passed through the dog.

The foundation of the Caleb Beach house, the oldest in Winchester. Beach sold it to Mrs. Filley. The remains were later moved to the Winchester green. *From the F.H. DeMars Collection.*

Proceeding farther, he saw the dog again and tried to kick harder but met only the same result. This happened repeatedly, his whole way home, and always with the dog disappearing before it could be struck. Rather than chalking the experience up to his activities at the Shingle House, the man knew this was the work of the witch Filley.

One thing that sets the stories of Mrs. Filley apart from those of other witches is that specific names are attached to them. For example, Benjamin W. Pettibone reported that a family had trouble getting butter to churn, until a wise old man told them to put a heated horseshoe into it. Doing so, Mrs. Filley immediately came to the house asking for a salve for a horseshoe shaped burn on her arm. Susan Serepta Beach remembered that when she was a young woman, she hung dresses on the line only to have one sleeve of each torn off horizontally. The great-grandmother of Frank DeMars, another Mrs. Beach, was a weaver of cloth who received an order on short notice. She borrowed a loom from Mrs. Filley with the promise to bring the loom back by noon on a given day. The loom worked well until noon on the last day, when she could get nothing to work. The family decided to bring the loom out to the woodshed, where the men looked it over for the cause of the trouble. Seeing nothing, they went inside to talk about it. The loom began running by itself. This bizarre occurrence reportedly happened twice. At this point, accounts of the story diverge. Some say that in frustration, Mrs. Beach decided she was done and pulled the fabric off, half a yard short. Others report that she called for Mrs. Filley, who happily helped Beach finish the job but said, "Thought ye could keep it longer than you promised did ye?"

· ·

Spindle Hill Road in Terryville becomes Witch Rock Road upon crossing into Bristol. This is a short distance from Fall Mountain, which was the reported home of a witch who pestered her Terryville neighbors in the late 1760s. Reports claimed that she was a member of the Albany circle of witches and would ride her aunt like a horse to the meetings. Town residents stated that they could feel hot coals and needles on their body when she was in the area. And then one day, the witch was gone. Rumors persist that she disappeared, fled might be the more accurate term, when the town announced it was going to begin prosecuting witches.

....

Legends like those of Moll Cramer, Molly Fisher, Mrs. Filley and Terryville's witch certainly are entertaining, but they also provide us with a window through which to observe the earliest days of Litchfield County's history. The experiences of these women perfectly illustrate John Demos's findings about witchcraft in eighteenth-century New England. Both Cramer and Fisher were poor, with little family and associated with thievery. Neither caused neighbors to fear for their lives; while Cramer certainly caused nuisances, Fisher was quite popular. The latter's dabbling with herbal medicine also fits the bill for eighteenth-century witches.

What both Cramer and Fisher represent is the danger present for women who stepped outside their ascribed gender roles. To eschew being an obedient wife and doting mother but rather live a life of independence was to risk being labeled a witch. While at an earlier time, the consequences might have been deadly for Cramer, Fisher and Filley, by the mid-eighteenth century, they simply became fodder for legends.

2
COUNTERFEITING

*I*f the stories of witches underscore the wildness that marked Litchfield County in its early years, then tales of counterfeiters certainly highlight the economic and legal difficulties the county faced. The extant record on counterfeiters in Litchfield County is exceedingly large, and an attempt to provide a definitive examination of this fascinating aspect of local history is beyond the scope of this book. Still, in exploring counterfeiting in the eighteenth and nineteenth centuries, important insights can be gained into the workings of the American economy in the colonial and early republic periods.

The counterfeiting craze that swept America between 1700 and 1865 had its origins in the shortages of coins, or specie, that led the American colonists to be the first people in the Western world to print paper money. This was primarily a function of the British mercantilist system, which severely limited the amount of gold and silver that could leave the mother country for the colonies. While foreign coins—especially those of Spain and Portugal—circulated, they were not enough to meet colonial demands. And when colonists began mining metals from which coins could be made, they were sternly reminded that the coining of money was exclusively a royal right.

The enterprising Americans, however, had other ideas for a means of exchange. First, they tried the wampum that served Native Americans so well. When that failed to gain widespread adoption, they attempted to use commodities as a source of money, with seventeenth-century Virginia adopting tobacco as an official currency and Massachusetts using corn.

Finally, in 1690, Massachusetts began printing bills of credit, which were really nothing more than a promise that future taxes would be levied to pay off debts. However, when the residents of Massachusetts began using them as paper currency, it appeared a solution to the lack of a practical means of exchange had been found. The ease of issuing such paper, coupled with the fact that the royal right extended only to metal coins, not paper, led other colonies to follow suit. Connecticut, for example, printed its first paper currency in 1704. These were bills of credit issued to offset the costs of war with France, and they used colored ink drawings of animals to discourage counterfeiting. In fact, paper currency was so popular that a 1764 British ban on such bills of credit was one of the factors that led to hostility between the British and their colonial subjects.

Several factors made counterfeiting so widespread. The foremost reason was the sheer number of different institutions that were issuing paper money, or notes. Each colony (later each state) issued its own, as did banks, insurance companies and even railroads. Any company that was chartered by the state had the right to issue paper money. This made it extraordinarily difficult to check the authenticity of currency; in fact, as historian Ben Tarnoff points out, by the time the federal government began issuing its own paper money during the Civil War, there were ten thousand different versions of paper notes from over two hundred institutions in circulation. The poor quality of these notes made them easy to counterfeit, and intercolonial rivalries and resentment made oversight and enforcement of anti-counterfeiting laws difficult. The result of this was that most counterfeiters fabricated currency from other states. Tarnoff has written that before the Civil War, a weak central government, "anarchic economic system" and the "irrepressible entrepreneurial spirit of its citizens helped make the country a haven for counterfeiters," who saw a chance to get rich quick, and to "fulfill the American Dream by making money, literally."

Still, most consumers were not especially bothered by the rash of counterfeiting; they were simply happy to have access to paper currency that they could exchange for needed goods and services. To obtain the legally preferred paper medium of exchange, banknotes, the consumer was required to have a bank account. And bank accounts were, in the eighteenth century, essentially the domain of the wealthy. To open a bank in the United Kingdom, a prospective customer needed to deposit fifty pounds, the rough equivalent of a month's wages for a craftsman. This was an enormous amount of money for the middle class and an impossible one for the poor. Such restrictions forced people to hide their money behind walls or bury it in their yards, but it also denied them access to paper money. Policies such as these led the general public to tolerate counterfeiters, who, it could be argued, were providing a service for the cash-strapped masses.

It was, perhaps, because counterfeiters filled this need that penalties for forging notes were actually reduced in the colonial era. In 1724, for example, Connecticut law mandated that a counterfeiter have his right ear cut off, have a large "C" branded on his forehead and be confined to a workhouse for life. Ten years later, that penalty was lowered to thirty lashes on the back with a whip, a large fine and ten years of imprisonment.

....

That significant numbers of Connecticut residents were willing to risk such punishments to make and distribute counterfeit currency speaks to the profits that stood to be made. No one personified these risks or rewards like Owen Sullivan, whose Dover Money Club produced enormous quantities of counterfeit notes in the disputed land between Litchfield County and New York's Dutchess County.

Sullivan was born in Ireland, most likely in the 1720s. He came to Massachusetts in 1742 as an indentured servant, trading four years of labor for passage to the New World. Conditions were so deplorable on the ship to America, however, that Sullivan agreed to add three years on to his period of indenture in exchange for all the biscuits he could eat in ninety minutes. Joining the Massachusetts militia, he was involved in the siege of Louisburg,

A counterfeit note drawn on the Wareham Bank, received by Litchfield's George Woodruff.
Collection of the Litchfield Historical Society, Litchfield, Connecticut.

In the bottom section of this writ, the Wareham Bank states that the note was made from a plate "bearing no resemblance to the genuine bills of this bank." *Collection of the Litchfield Historical Society, Litchfield, Connecticut.*

Canada, and with the British victory remained there for several years, honing his metalworking skills, marrying and becoming a heavy drinker. As Sullivan described his marital situation, "I unhappily married a wife, which proved a torment to me, and made my life uncomfortable, and she was given to take a cup too much, and I for my part took to the same." The Sullivans settled in Boston, where Owen worked as a silversmith, an occupation that gave him ample practice in engraving the plates with which currency was made.

Sullivan thus embarked on a seven-year career as one of history's most famous counterfeiters. He possessed qualities essential in the field: he was both a master engraver and a master in gaining the trust of others. Sullivan's career also highlights the pyramidal structure of those involved in counterfeiting. By far the most important link in the chain was the role performed by Sullivan, that of the engraver. To make the plates, engravers needed to replicate the smallest details of the note *backward* on a piece of metal. Next were the printers, who needed to match the type of paper and color of ink. Finally, to keep the different links in the chain separate, counterfeiting rings employed passers to circulate their money. These men often sold the notes at a discounted rate, either purchasing their supply from the engraver and printer or working on consignment.

It was a fight with his wife that led to Sullivan's first arrest. In a drunken shouting match, Mrs. Sullivan screamed, "You forty-thousand-pound moneymaker!" This confirmed the suspicions of others, who had long thought that the ink on the money used by Sullivan was too black. He was arrested on August 28, 1749, with more than thirty counterfeit Massachusetts notes on him. Searching his home, authorities found printing materials, ink and scraps of paper with Sullivan's attempts to forge the signatures of colonial officials. Convicted in 1750 of "wickedly falsely & deceptively forging" Massachusetts bills, Sullivan was locked in the pillory at the Old State House for two hours and whipped twenty times.

Fleeing Boston, Sullivan moved on to Rhode Island and forged its notes for the next two years. That currency was notoriously easy to counterfeit, and this, combined with the colony's extraordinarily weak government, made its currency a favorite for colonial counterfeiters. It didn't take long for Sullivan to make his mark. A Boston newspaper declared that his work was "exceedingly well counterfeited, so that without inspecting very narrowly, few but what may be deceived." That this article was reprinted in at least two other newspapers in New York and Massachusetts meant that Sullivan was gaining a reputation across the colonies. Perhaps this made the Irishman a particular target for the authorities, for in September 1752 he was again convicted of counterfeiting. Pilloried for ninety minutes, he was also branded with an "R" for "incorrigible rogue," an appellation saved only for those men deemed beyond redemption. Sullivan, ever the charmer, did manage to convince his jailer to brand him above the hairline, where it was less obvious. Arrested with an accomplice, Sullivan asked to be able to watch his associate be punished. In reality, Sullivan used this as an opportunity to escape. He fled Providence and trekked 150 miles across Rhode Island and Connecticut and settled in the disputed area along the New York/Connecticut border known as the Oblong.

The Oblong was a two-mile-wide, sixty-mile-long tract of iron ore–rich land. While this had been ceded to New York in 1731 in exchange for the piece of land in southwestern Connecticut that is now Greenwich and Stamford, Connecticut had never agreed to the exact position of the boundary line; in fact, the monument marking the point where Connecticut, New York and Massachusetts meet denotes the location of the latter two states but not Connecticut, as the Nutmeg State never agreed to the boundary.

It was in this land, where neither state could agree on who was responsible for enforcing the law, that Sullivan began the third leg of his counterfeiting career. He settled in Dover, a collection of villages and farm communities that included portions of what is now Kent. Both the people and the geography played to Sullivan's advantage. Mostly German immigrants, the settlers simply wanted to be left alone. They cared little for what their neighbors were doing. And the mountains, swamps and forests—not to mention the wolves and mountain lions for which the local governments had put out bounties—provided places to hide and obstacles to pursuers.

And there were caves. Sullivan made his headquarters in one that he outfitted with wood panels, flooring and furniture. Here, Sullivan established a gang and set about producing thousands of pounds of counterfeit currency that would make him the bane of at least three colonies—Connecticut, New York and Rhode Island—whose currencies were so debased by Sullivan's work that they offered a four-hundred-pound reward for his capture.

Sullivan was experienced enough to know that a counterfeiter could not stay in one place for very long. He traveled frequently, producing fake bills wherever he went. The engraver's dilemma was that he was reliant upon many unsavory characters to pass his money into the mainstream economy. Unfortunately for Sullivan, when those he came across were questioned by authorities, they quickly passed along the engraver's name. When a Robert Clarke caught on to a Sullivan-led scam, he was offered a fortune in counterfeit bills, but Clarke instead provided law enforcement with details about the workings of what was becoming known as the Dover Money Club. Shutting down the club would require someone willing to take the information from these passers and work his way up the pyramid.

Sullivan moved too easily between Dover and Kent for either Connecticut or New York to apprehend him alone, and the disagreements between the two colonies over the Oblong ensured that they wouldn't cooperate. An individual, however, was willing to tackle the problem himself. Eliphalet Beecher was a forty-year-old merchant and New Haven native who offered to hunt down Sullivan if the Connecticut and New York legislatures would pay his expenses and give him a reward. When New York refused to charge or extradite people he arrested, the Connecticut legislature issued a statement regretting "many difficulties" caused by "want of the encouragement and assistance of the civil authority" of New York and further asked that Connecticut's governor write his New York counterpart and demand full cooperation.

Even with the two colonies arguing over his jurisdiction, Beecher proceeded to lay a trap for Sullivan. He enlisted the services of a tavern keeper, who led Beecher to the furnished cave. Evidence gathered there led them to a house, which appeared empty. Beecher, however, did such a thorough search of the premises that he found loose floorboards under a bed, which, when removed, revealed a tunnel that led to a burrow that housed Sullivan. This burrow was on Preston Mountain, in Kent. Sullivan surrendered and initially tried to

A rough wood carving of the execution of Owen Sullivan. Note that the image depicts the short drop gallows. *Courtesy American Antiquarian Society.*

bribe his way out before confessing to making hundreds of thousands of pounds of currency.

Beecher brought his quarry to New Haven, where colonial officials decided to extradite the prisoner to the New York colony. This was because Connecticut law allowed only for branding, cropping ears and sentencing to the workhouse, while New York law specified hanging for counterfeiters. Thus it was that Sullivan was led to the gallows on St. Patrick's Day 1756. There, in the last moments of his life, Sullivan outlined his illicit accomplishments, claiming to have made ten to twelve thousand pounds of New Hampshire currency, three thousand pounds of Connecticut's, vast quantities of New York's and virtually uncountable amounts of Rhode Island currency. This was at a time when a single pound could purchase ten gallons of rum. Sullivan also said he hoped his accomplices would also hang, "but I will not betray them, or be guilty of shedding their blood." He did, however, hope that they would destroy the plates and money, so "that they may not die on a tree as I do." He finally uttered his last words, "Don't pull the rope so tight—it is hard for a man to die in cold blood."

....

Connecticut continued to suffer heavily from Sullivan's fake bills for years, which caused great concern to the government and merchants alike. And while most of Sullivan's club escaped, many were caught. In 1752, Benjamin Force was arrested in Sharon for passing a fake Rhode Island three-pound note; he at first maintained his innocence but then turned state's witness against the Dover Money Club. Two years later, Jehiel Murray of Merryall was convicted of passing fake Rhode Island notes, and his fellow townsmen David Owen and Samuel Cogswell were convicted of the same offense and of counterfeiting copper coins from pewter. They had cast half and quarter pieces of eight. For these offenses they were flogged thirty-nine times. Samuel Little of Litchfield was sentenced to jail for passing fake Rhode Island currency.

In 1755, Amos Tyler of Sharon was arrested for passing fake Rhode Island currency. He promised that he would search "day and night" for the man who gave him the bills and in so doing convinced the assembly to reduce his punishment. David Ensign of New Hartford was also arrested for passing fake Rhode Island currency. The following year, Ebeneezer Jackson Jr. of Sharon (who was married to Abigail Tyler, who may have been Amos Tyler's twin) was charged with passing counterfeit money and perjury. Initially held on a 160-pound bond, he asked to have this reduced, as it would ruin his father. Jackson later submitted a statement alleging that his indiscretions were due to poor judgment and confusion rather than malicious intent, and he even included a certificate of good behavior and repentance signed by thirty-one residents of Sharon along with testimony from pastors that he had made a public confession apology and was "living acceptably to the church." A likely accomplice of Tyler and Jackson's was Caleb Strong of Sharon. Although never convicted of passing or possessing notes, he was arrested for perjury. In August 1756, another member of the Dover Money Club, Joseph Steele, was tried in Litchfield and admitted passing a phony forty-shilling note to the wife of Benjamin Gaylord of New Milford.

....

The colonists' proclivity toward counterfeiting was used against them during the Revolutionary War, when the British employed a strategy of utilizing fake currency to destabilize the American economy. This worked with devastating effects. In fact, the value of a 1778 continental dollar fell to twenty-five cents, and by 1779 it was worth only a nickel. Two of Britain's master counterfeiters had a Litchfield County connection. Israel and Isaac Young ran a counterfeiting operation on Long Island falsifying Connecticut's twenty-shilling bill. Arrested by a group of minutemen who stormed Isaac's house, they were held in the jail that stood on what is now East Street in Litchfield.

After the war, the Americans were loath to learn lessons from their colonial counterfeiting experiences, and money problems continued into the early republic era. During and in the immediate wake of the war, Congress printed too much paper money, which led to a collapse in its value. The nation's first instrument of government, the Articles of Confederation, permitted states to continue to print paper money and neglected to give Congress power to stop the counterfeiting of state notes. Thus, in 1786, selectmen in the town of Kent were authorized to settle with Colonel Andrew Adams to "grant such relief as they think for the counterfeit bills he has taken for the state rates."

Furthermore, with the value of paper money plunging, states—most notably Massachusetts—passed laws requiring taxes be paid in specie, to which farmers often lacked access. This led directly to Shays' Rebellion, which attempted to close down courthouses in order to prevent the seizure of delinquent farms. In the spring of 1787, Dr. John Hurlbert of Alford,

A satire of issues facing Connecticut on the eve of the Constitutional Convention. Note that the second figure from the right at the top of the page is proclaiming, "Success to Shays." *Library of Congress.*

Massachusetts, a supporter of Shays, arrived in Sharon to awaken a "similar spirit." Hurlbert organized a number of men under William Mitchell, who as captain trained his company in secret. Hurlbert, Mitchell and three others were arrested, but when Shays' Rebellion collapsed, the prosecutions were discontinued. The danger to the new government was clear, however, and later that year the Constitutional Convention met in Philadelphia. Still, the inability of the young American government to effectively deal with its monetary problems led to a golden age of counterfeiting highlighted by Litchfield County's William Stuart.

••••••••••••••••••••

William Stuart was born a farmer's son in Wilton, Connecticut, in 1788. Much of what is known of him comes from his autobiography, a rollicking tale published in 1854, which if accepted as largely true provides a detailed accounting of one of nineteenth-century America's great lives of crime. On the title page, Stuart promised "startling details of daring feats performed by himself—perils by sea and land—frequent arrests and imprisonment—blowing out of jail with powder—failure of escape after he had led his cowardly associates out the terrible pit," and he didn't disappoint.

Stuart described his ten-year-old self as a "demi-devil," so angry and wild that he retaliated against his teacher, Edward Coburn, for "thrash[ing] me almost daily" by throwing Coburn's son into a "large quantity of semi-liquid manure, and after two or three ineffectual efforts to extricate himself, he rose upon his feet, a hideous specimen of pollution. I

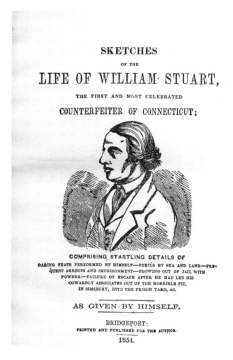

SKETCHES
OF THE
LIFE OF WILLIAM STUART,
THE FIRST AND MOST CELEBRATED
COUNTERFEITER OF CONNECTICUT;

COMPRISING STARTLING DETAILS OF
DARING FEATS PERFORMED BY HIMSELF—PERILS BY SEA AND LAND—FRE-
QUENT ARRESTS AND IMPRISONMENT—BLOWING OUT OF JAIL WITH
POWDER—FAILURE OF ESCAPE AFTER HE HAD LED HIS
COWARDLY ASSOCIATES OUT OF THE HORRIBLE PIT,
IN SIMSBURY, INTO THE PRISON YARD, &C.

AS GIVEN BY HIMSELF.

BRIDGEPORT:
PRINTED AND PUBLISHED FOR THE AUTHOR.
1854.

William Stuart, from the cover of his autobiography. *From* Sketches of the Life of William Stuart, the First and Most Celebrated Counterfeiter of Connecticut.

started for home, and laughed heartily at his inglorious situation." He continued to engage in a series of "frolics," which he funded by counterfeiting coins out of pewter, and by altering legal coins into ones with greater value: "I took pieces of sole leather and enclosed the silver between them, and with a shoe hammer upon a lap stone, beat over the centre of the coin, and in three minutes, sixpences became shillings, and shillings became quarters. But this sort was not enough. I melted pewter, and run it in moulds, and thus I could coin one hundred quarters in an evening." Stuart continued with this minor counterfeiting operation even after his father died, leaving the burgeoning criminal with a $3,000 inheritance.

By sixteen, however, Stuart had moved on to more serious crimes, including throwing a prostitute into a fire. When brought before a judge, he proclaimed, "I had read of burnt offerings to the Lord, and it was my intention, by…throwing her upon the fire, to make a burnt offering to the Devil." Stuart had to dip into his inheritance to pay the fine and soon left Connecticut for what he thought would be the more exciting environs of Pennsylvania.

His conjecture was correct, and Stuart remembered 1804 as a year of "rowdyism, drunkenness, profanity, gambling, and debaucheries." The following year, he returned to Connecticut and, while at a tavern with a friend, had an encounter that would have profound consequences for Stuart. A stranger approached the two and

> appealed to our honor again, to keep our transactions hidden from the view of the people, and swore to keep his revelations secret. He now took from his person a roll of bank bills; told us they were counterfeit and offered to sell us some of them. Neither of us understood what counterfeit money was, he explained it to our satisfaction and now we saw how suddenly we could become rich—have our pockets lined with gold, and live in affluence and ease…He engaged to furnish us for ten dollars a hundred, any quantity that we wished…Was not here golden bait? What greater inducements could be laid before the senses of an ambitious and unscrupulous youth?

Stuart sold his horse and saddle for $35, bought $350 worth of counterfeit bills and was delighted to find that merchants accepted them. He was hooked and spent decades of his life heavily invested as a passer of counterfeit currency.

He became part of a pyramid run out of Canada. The engraver at the top of the organization was William Crane. Stuart would bring the latest examples of paper money north of the border for Crane to replicate. He also brought the latest counterfeit detecting aids to alert the engraver to common mistakes. Within a week, Crane would have made a plate and enough copies would have been made to send Stuart back to Connecticut. On one trip alone, Stuart returned with $40,000 in counterfeit currency with him.

Worried that Connecticut authorities were on his tail, he moved first to Philadelphia and then to Baltimore, where the law caught up to him. He escaped with the flair that marked most episodes in Stuart's life. A woman Stuart hired to help with his operations visited the prison and presented her colleague with a supply of gunpowder, which Stuart used to blast his way out of his cell. He made a quick escape to Connecticut.

Back in the Nutmeg State, he visited a cousin who had just married, and "he and his wife over-persuaded me and her sister to get married. I was rather reluctant, and so was she, but they talked us into it. So we were married and enjoyed life as well as others." The newly married rogue attempted to live a reformed life but later confessed that his "rambling propensities drove me away in speculation again." This time, Stuart wrote:

> *I was the chief of the gang—the planner of operations, and more thoroughly versed in the tactics of roguery than any of them. Hence they looked to me as a guide; but I was not elated by this distinction. I was bold, fearless, and daring, yet cautious, circumspect, and wary, and so constituted by nature as by any unexpected emergency. I instinctively, without premeditation, was sure to adopt the best plan, and execute my purposes in such a way as experience proved to be the best. I was gifted with unusual powers of self-possession, I was never disconcerted but calm and deliberate or wild and turbulent, as occasion seemed to require.*

Stuart's gang numbered about six people, each working toward a general plan. Stuart remembered that they "rode about the country, bought watches, jockeyed horses, bought sheep, and other stock, paying for them chiefly in counterfeit money. My bank was strong and for years it failed not. When we were rapidly lessening our stock, one of the firm went to Canada and returned with a supply." Stuart's favorite place to pass money was at militia musters, where the large quantities of alcohol present made the would-be soldiers less likely to question the authenticity of the money.

Still, Stuart looked to remove himself from a life of crime. He moved his family to Bridgewater "to get away from my associates, and this gang of counterfeiters. This removal did not avail me, for rogues will find each other, if they are separated by oceans and continents." In fact, his attempt at living a clean lifestyle didn't even last long enough for him to arrive in Bridgewater. On the move, he passed counterfeit money at least nine places. After he had moved to Bridgewater, he hid his Canadian counterfeited money in local caves in his new hometown and in Roxbury, including Raven Rock, which was also used by counterfeiter Steve Rance and his Gamaliel Gang.

Stuart's schemes seemingly became more audacious as time passed. He ran a scam in which he "sold" his body servant Pomp, only to have the latter run away and meet Stuart at a preordained location, where they would split the money. During the War of 1812, Stuart served as a recruiting agent and pocketed the real money the government gave him as bounties for soldiers while paying out bounties in counterfeit money. The widespread use of counterfeit money for bounties led to a change in the law requiring recruits to be paid in specie. Stuart responded by purchasing real one-dollar notes from banks and using chemicals to remove the "1," which he replaced with a "20," "50" or "100," which he then brought to a bank to exchange for specie.

Leaving for Georgia (where he intended to carry out a series of crimes) Sullivan was arrested, ironically enough, for inadvertently passing a counterfeit bill in Ridgefield. Known to be a mere runner—albeit a particularly audacious one—in a counterfeit pyramid, he was offered clemency if he'd name his accomplices, but Sullivan refused. He was sentenced to a term in Newgate Prison in East Granby. His exploits continued, even behind bars. Assigned a quota of making an average of eight pounds of nails a day, Stuart calculated that he could do this work in only six months, so he spent time drinking rum instead of working. These antics earned him a stay in solitary confinement. To secure the rum in the first place, Stuart counterfeited coins out of pewter. He plotted escapes—all unsuccessful—and led an insurrection. Injured in the fight, he pretended to be more hurt than he was to get early release.

In 1854, at sixty-six years old, Stuart published his autobiography. He hoped it would "stand as a beacon to warn the young and ambitious against vice and crime…to warn men inclined to criminal courses, of the unmitigated evils attendant upon a willful disregard of honesty, public morality and legal enactments." One wonders, however, if his tales of daring and drama didn't have the opposite effect.

....

Stuart's renunciation of the rogue's lifestyle did not end counterfeiting in Litchfield County. In 1858, four years after Stuart wrote his autobiography, the Litchfield Bank was declared insolvent. This bank had been incorporated a mere two years earlier and had actually been in business only since 1857. Testimony regarding the bankruptcy revealed that the bank had paid nearly $1,000 in several transactions to the firm of Monroe, Dye and Taylor. John S. Dye was the editor of the *Government Counterfeiting Detector*, a bimonthly guide to determining the legitimacy of money. Their services were retained with the unrealized hope "not to blow the bank" through the sheer volume of counterfeit Litchfield Bank notes that were floated. In fact, at the time of this writing, Heritage Auctions, an online auction company, has several counterfeit Litchfield Bank notes for sale.

Two years later, in February 1860, J.L. Van Wert, a former worker at Winsted's Gilbert Clock, and his young sister-in-law were arrested in a hotel in Southwick, Massachusetts. The *Winsted Herald* had earlier reported that Van Wert had gained control of a gold mine in Canada and that the notes he was passing around town were the fruits of this operation. In actuality, he was passing counterfeit notes from the fabricated Still River Bank in town. He was using large bills to purchase small meals at local taverns and pocketing the real change. The notes listed Van Wert as the bank president and his sister-in-law as the cashier. When the notes were brought to town for redemption, they were, of course, rejected. Van Wert was sentenced to six years in prison.

The Civil War, with its explosion in the size and power of the federal government, brought an end to the golden age of counterfeiting. In June 1865, the Secret Service was established, with its initial charge being to combat the wave of counterfeiting brought on by the federal government's issuance of the paper currency known as "greenbacks." This new agency was so effective that by the end of the nineteenth century, counterfeit currency had been slashed to only a tiny fraction of what was in circulation. Thus, those wishing to illegally make a living by manipulating Litchfield County's financial infrastructure had to turn to more traditional means, like scams and robbing banks.

....

A remarkable advertisement appeared in the August 23, 1827 edition of the *Litchfield County Post*. It told of a subscriber who planned on "erecting in the Village of Litchfield, Conn. By the first day of September next an AERIAL PHAETON." He promised to provide "an agreeable pastime to Ladies and Gentleman," which in itself didn't sound exciting. That pastime, however, consisted of "four Carriages, each supported by two Arms, which are attached to an Axle-tree in the centre. They are turned by a Propelling Machine, and will carry Eight persons at once, two in each Carriage, who will in regular succession be raised to the distance of fifty feet in the air, at a rate and velocity equal to ten miles a minute, or slower, as suits the wishes of those occupying the carriages, and all with perfect ease and safety."

A flying machine that would thrill its passenger with speeds of up to six hundred miles per hour! Nothing like this had been imagined, never mind operated. The advertisement even spoke of endorsements: "This method of recreation and amusement, has been highly recommended by the most eminent physicians in the United States, and will be found the best mode of

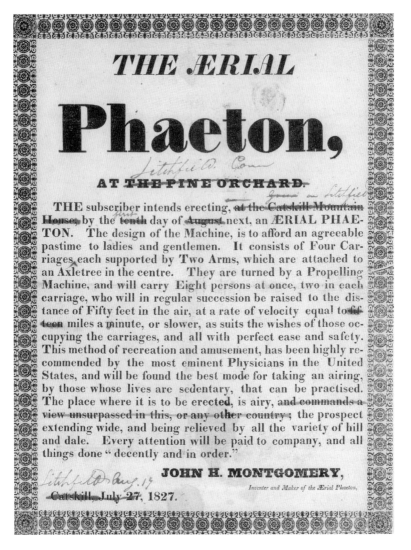

An advertisement for the aerial phaeton. Note how the ad was altered for distribution in the Litchfield newspaper. *Collection of the Litchfield Historical Society, Litchfield, Connecticut.*

taking an airing, by those whose lives are sedentary, that can be practiced." All this could be had for the reasonable price of twelve and a half cents per ride, half price for children.

Wicked can come with a sense of humor. And while this may have been the nineteenth-century version of spam involving a Nigerian prince, it was certainly creative enough to catch the eye. Unlike those anonymous charlatans, the aerial phaeton was the work of "a Shirtless rascal by the name of JOHN H. MONTGOMERY." Montgomery was exposed as a swindler in the September 13 edition of the paper. He had visited Litchfield—"whether in an aerial or a more humble phaeton, the deponent saith not"—to "sponge a few of our citizens." The notice went so far as to say that Montgomery's "soft white hand proves that he prefers to live by sponging rather than by honest labor." Furthermore, the paper learned that this was not Montgomery's "first or second exploit of the kind."

It is unknown whether the law ever caught up with Montgomery, who was deemed to be a "citizen of the world." Regardless, the modest wickedness that he brought to Litchfield County speaks to the types of scams that existed in this era of counterfeiting.

....

The Winsted Bank was founded in 1849 and by 1861 was located in a multistory building next to the Second Congregational Church on Main Street. Here the bank occupied the first floor and rented out upper-story offices. In the area immediately above the bank's vault was the office of lawyer V.R.C. Giddings, a New Milford native. According to some sources, Giddings's offices were empty in November 1861.

The bank's security apparatus was impressive for the time period. The vault, on four sides, was built of thick granite slabs, and two feet of cinders underneath the floorboards provided protection from fire. The vault could be accessed only through iron-plated doors. However, at nine o'clock on the morning of Monday, November 11, Henry Gay, a teller who later became the bank president, discovered that the bank had been robbed.

Over $60,000—a value approaching $2,000,000 in the twenty-first century—was taken from the vault, "without a trace," as the event was reported in the *New York Times*. Over $50,000 of the stolen sum was in the form of Winsted Bank notes. It is interesting to note that the culprits clearly understood some of the finer intricacies of the nineteenth-century banking system, for they only stole about half of the Winsted Bank notes. Had they purloined all of them, the bank would certainly have collapsed and the notes rendered worthless. The remainder of the haul was in the form of United States Treasury notes, gold and silver coins, notes from other banks and over $1,000 in notes from the Hurlburt Bank, which at one time rented space above the Winsted Bank.

The area around Robbers' Cave, where the break-in of the Winsted Bank was planned. *From the F.H. DeMars Collection.*

In the wake of the robbery, reports came in that several men had been living in a network of caves south of town for a few weeks. (This is now called Robber's Cave, and is visible today above the Winsted branch of the Department of Motor Vehicles.) Hunters saw the men there—and later stated that they could identify the culprits if apprehended—and at night fires could be seen from town. Cooking utensils left behind by the perpetrators were later recovered by detectives.

It was, perhaps, these perpetrators who were the strangers seen carrying large carpetbags into town on the night of November 9. An 1862 edition of *Bankers Magazine* described how the robbery took place:

> *The thieves had evidently studied the localities with great care, and undertook their work with a degree of circumspection and skill seldom exhibited by the profession. They entered through a lawyer's office, which was directly over the vault of the bank. Boards in the floor, of unequal length, were neatly sawed through, and after proceeding with the work in the vault, they were carefully replaced, screwed down, puttied over, and then sanded, so as not to attract observation. The enclosure of the vault was of granite, the top slab being over six inches thick. Through this they chiseled their way, splitting it in two, raising off one-half of it, and thus affording room to descend into the vault. On retiring with their booty they replaced the stone, screwed down the floor, and left everything in such apple-pie order that it took the bank officers some time to discover the mysterious hole through which their treasure had departed.*

Later reports differed as to whether the men had a skeleton key to Attorney Gidding's office or whether they picked the lock with sharpened nails that were left behind at the scene. Ashes were used to muffle the noise of drilling through the first five inches of the eight-inch-thick granite slab with a ratchet drill. Lead deadened the sound of the chiseling described in the article.

A reward of $1,000 was immediately offered, but the only lead was that three men had been seen at the tollgate on Greenwoods Turnpike between Winsted and Norfolk. This report stated that the men were carrying carpetbags that they continually switched between hands, which would be consistent with making off with the approximately two hundred pounds the money would have weighed. Rumors surfaced that some silver, amounting perhaps to $18,000, was stashed in a stone wall and later recovered.

There are apparently no records as to whether those who carried out the heist were ever convicted. One theory holds that the bank, realizing it would not recover any additional money from the heist, did not push for prosecution as it had promised a $1,000 reward for bringing the perpetrators to justice. Thus, a successful prosecution would only cost the bank additional money.

Still, the Winsted Bank never recovered. Whereas it had been once been on its way to being a leading regional financial institution, it closed seven years after the robbery.

3

GALLOWS LANE

Crime and Punishment in Litchfield County

*P*lace names are often guides to a town's past. Dog Pond in Goshen, for example, gained its name in 1738 when Deacon Nathaniel Baldwin's canine drowned there. In Litchfield's case, this is perhaps most graphically illustrated with Gallows Lane. Famed as a grueling test of endurance in the final miles of the Litchfield Hills Road Race, most town residents have heard the story that the street got its name because executions once took place there. The historian—trained to be a skeptic—questions this piece of lore. But it's true. And the stories behind these executions reveal crimes of a bloody nature we don't often associate with our forefathers or life in a quiet Connecticut county.

· · · · · · · · · · · · · · · · · · · ·

It is important to note that into the nineteenth century, the laws of Litchfield County were dominated by the religious regulations of the county's Puritan fathers. With no separation of church and state in Connecticut until 1818 (and with some towns remaining intertwined with the Congregational Church until the following decade), ministers performed important roles in advising or even participating in town governments. As historian Michael-John Cavallaro has written, "On the frontier of Colonial America, the acting law was God's Law, or at least God's Law as interpreted by a minister and the colonial court system."

Blasphemy and adultery were serious crimes, and a central tenet of punishment for these crimes was public shaming, which most often meant the pillory, whipping, branding and physical mutilation.

....

Perhaps the quintessential images of justice in colonial America are the stocks and the pillory. The stocks were a wooden device used to lock up the feet, legs or ankles. As early as 1773, Goshen selectmen were instructed to erect both a public signpost and a "pair of stocks nearby." The pillory refers to a specific punitive device, different from the stocks. In a pillory, a wooden or metal frame was used to secure a prisoner by the head and wrists, rendering him immobile and—since the angle was specifically calculated—in great pain. A crowd would then be free to add to the prisoner's distress by throwing stones, dung or fruit at him or even perhaps personally striking him.

Whipping would be used as a punishment for more serious crimes. State laws—and military code—typically forbade general courts and sheriffs from administering more than forty lashes, so it was common for a prisoner to be whipped thirty-nine times. Most towns had a whipping post to which the prisoner would be tied.

Torrington's whipping post was used primarily for those convicted of stealing. In 1817 and again in 1818, constable Israel Cox oversaw the whipping of convicts, one for stealing broadcloth from a mill, the other for stealing a silver spoon from a home. In 1830, Nelson Flyer of Torrington appeared in court to answer charges that he "did feloniously take, steal, and carry away one certain gold finger ring with a stone set therein of the value of ten dollars" from Ransom Hine. Found guilty, Flyer was ordered to return the ring and pay a fine of $5.00 (which would be tripled for punitive purposes) plus $9.30 for the cost of the prosecution. When Flyer refused to pay, he was, according to Justice of the Peace Russell Abernathy, "punished by whipping four stripes on his naked body and pay costs of prosecution and stand committed till this judgment be complied with." Tradition holds that while Flyer was whipped, he escaped before he could be imprisoned.

Litchfield utilized multiple methods of whipping its convicts. In front of the jail stood the Whipping Post Elm, a notable piece of the town's arboreal history. The tree was believed to have been planted in 1720, the year Litchfield was settled, and for many years served a role in punishing the town's criminals. In 1779, George Pitkin, clerk of the Litchfield Court, signed an order stating

Litchfield's Whipping Post Elm. *Collection of the Litchfield Historical Society, Litchfield, Connecticut.*

that "if any person within this state shall presume willfully to blaspheme the name of God the Father, Son or Holy Ghost, either by denying, cursing or reproaching the true God, or his government of the World; every person so offending shall be punished by whipping on the naked body, not exceeding forty stripes, and sitting in the pillory one hour."

In carrying out punishments for horse stealing, the Litchfield court ordered that prisoners "be twice set astride a wooden horse and kept there an hour and then whipped fifteen stripes on the naked body, with an interval of a month between the two punishments."

Litchfield employed specific means to ensure that the shaming associated with whipping was as public as possible. A wagon was used to transport the prisoner around town, so that many different people could witness the punishment. This was the sentence carried out against Samuel Tousley, a wealthy resident of the town, in 1779. Tousley was branded on the forehead with a capital "B," marking him as a blasphemer. He was then "tied to a tail of a Cart, and caused him to be whip'd thirty-nine Stripes in his Naked body, in the whole,—at four of the most public places in the Town of Litchfield and then returned to the Gaol from whence he came."

An additional aspect of Tousley's punishment hints at a more extreme form of punishment. Prior to being branded and whipped, Tousley was taken from the jail to a gallows and "set him thereon with a Rope round his Neck for the space of one full hour." This must have been both terrifying and deterring. In 1804, John Landon, sheriff of Litchfield County, reported:

Whereas Samuel Whitmore, of New Milford, in said county before the Superior Court holden at Litchfield in said county, on the 1st Tuesday of February 1804, was legally convicted of Adultery, and on consideration, was by the Judges of said Court sentenced and adjudged to be whipped on his naked body Ten Stripes, and to be stigmatized or burnt on his forehead with the letter "A" on a hot iron, and to wear a halter about his neck on the outside of his garments during his abode in this State of Connecticut—and as often as he shall be found without his said halter, worn as aforesaid, upon information and proof of the same before any Assistant of Justice of the Peace, to be whipped not exceeding thirty stripes, and to pay the cost of this prosecution.

The justice of the peace referenced in the above account was the main law enforcement officer of the towns that made up the county. They had the power to issue citations and arrest people. Once someone was arrested, however, he became the responsibility of the Litchfield County sheriff. The sheriff was responsible for maintaining the jail, transporting prisoners to and from the jail and court and collecting fines. He also supervised—often with assistance—the physical punishments ordered by the court. Lynde Lorde, born in Lyme in 1733, was the second and perhaps the most notable sheriff in Litchfield County's history, serving thirty years, from 1771 until his death in 1801.

It was Lorde who, in February 1776, wrote, "I caused the within named John Thomas to be taken from the common Gaol in Litchfield to the place of Execution and there Set upon a Gallos with a Rope Round his Neck for the full Term of one hour and Then tied to the Tail of a Cart and Transported to four of the most public places in the Town of Litchfield and there whipped on his naked body Thirty-nine stripes in the whole." Lorde also collected a forty-shilling fine from Thomas. This particular form of punishment raises the question of whether Lorde actually commuted a death sentence while Thomas was on the gallows.

. . . .

The gallows was not only employed as a means of scaring convicts straight, however. Since 1636, 126 people have been executed in Connecticut, 107 of them by hanging, which was the method of execution from 1639 to 1936. At different points in the state's history, Connecticut has held the death penalty out as the punishment for arson, piracy, treason, murder, sodomy, rape, horse stealing, slave rebellion, counterfeiting and witchcraft. Of Connecticut's documented executions, four took place in Litchfield, three of them on Gallows Lane.

. . . .

The first of those executed was John Jacob, a Native American. Of the first ten men executed for homicide in Connecticut, seven were Native Americans. Jacob's victim was James Chokerer, a member of the Schaghticoke tribe living in Kent. On February 17, 1768, Jacob, a resident of Farmington, was paying a visit to Chokerer and his wife when things between the two men became heated. In the midst of an argument, Jacob called his friend "a damned Schatacook" and, grabbing a hatchet, killed Chokerer. A trial was held at which Jacob was very quickly found "guilty without mitigating factors." On November 2, 1768, a gallows was erected along Middle Street (now Gallows Lane) in Litchfield, which up to that point was notable only as the widest street (28 rods, or 154 feet) in town. The Reverend Timothy Pitkin was asked to preach a sermon to the condemned, and addressing Jacob directly, he proclaimed, "Prisoner Attend! You deserve to suffer the eternal pains of hell!" The trapdoor soon sprung, and Jacob fell to his death.

....

The confrontation between Jacob and Chokerer was not the first instance of violence in the county targeting or committed by Native Americans. During a conflict in 1708, the Reverend Anthony Stoddard of Woodbury was walking in his garden after church services had concluded one Sunday evening. While passing near the Cranberry Pond, he caught a glimpse of a Native American hiding in the bushes. Entering his house, Stoddard took his gun, "obtained a fair view of him, fired, and the Indian fell." Stoddard immediately returned to his home, but the next morning upon investigating the results of his shot, he—in the words of the county history—"discovered another red foe near his companion, whom he also dispatched."

The fear of attacks by Native Americans was evident in the early architecture of Litchfield County's towns. In Litchfield between 1720 and 1730, five houses were surrounded by palisades, a fence made of wooden stakes or tree trunks and used for defensive purposes. One of these was at the site of the current courthouse, while three others were located south, east and west of town. The fifth was located in the part of town then known as South Farms, now the town of Morris. A house in Goshen was also palisaded, and a history of that town provides a description of the defensive work:

> They dug a deep ditch around the house, placed logs perpendicularly in it all around the house, leaving a space only for a gate. The logs were placed close together, sharpened at the top, and extended eight, ten or twelve feet above the ground. The earth taken from the trench was then returned, and beaten down until the logs stood firmly; and this, with a gate well secured, was a tolerable defense against a sudden attack from the Indians.

No description was left as to how the defense in Goshen was manned, but in Litchfield, soldiers—probably militiamen—manned the palisades while the town's residents worked in the fields or attended Sunday worship.

Still, these defenses only protected those residents who were within their reach. In May 1722, Captain Jacob Griswold of Litchfield was working alone in a field one mile west of the center of town when he was captured by two Native Americans. By the end of that day, Griswold had been brought to what is now Canaan but was then an unsettled wilderness. His captors bound Griswold's hands and feet, started a fire and then fell asleep. Griswold was able to escape his bindings, take his captors' firearms and head off into the woods. The Native Americans awoke and began a pursuit, but when they came upon Griswold, he held them back with the weapons. Their quest to recapture the one-time prisoner continued until Griswold reached approximately the current intersection of Route 63 and Norfolk Road, where he fired one of his weapons, alerting the townspeople and bringing them to his assistance.

Joseph Harris was not as lucky. In 1723, Harris, known as a "respectable inhabitant" of Litchfield, was attacked by a group of Native Americans very near where Griswold was taken captive. When Harris attempted to escape, he was shot dead and scalped. Residents searched the area when Harris did not return to town that afternoon, but darkness put an end to their efforts. The next morning, his body was found, sitting on the ground, his head resting against a tree. He was the first of

WEST CEMETERY—JOSEPH HARRIS

A memorial erected in Litchfield's West Cemetery to Joseph Harris, killed by Native Americans. The monument was erected in 1830, evidence of the town's early appreciation for its own history. The marker still stands but is now illegible. *From* Litchfield and Morris Inscriptions.

Litchfield's original settlers to die. His burial spot is long forgotten, but in 1830 a memorial was erected to Harris in the town's West Cemetery.

•••••••••••••••••••••

A particularly unusual and political murder took place in Washington during the Revolutionary War. The Davies' Hollow section of town was a hotbed for Tories, and the town's patriots gathered at the home of John Logan to decide how best to dislodge these loyalists. While they were discussing options, Logan went to a neighbor's house and returned with a musket. His sister asked him what he planned to do with the weapon. "Shoot Tories!" her brother responded. "You shoot Tories!" she chastised him. "You haven't pluck enough to fire the gun." Logan insisted he had, and when the sister remarked, "Then shoot me," he fired and killed her instantly.

....

One of the county's most brutal crimes, the killing of the Mallory family of Washington by Barnett Davenport in 1780, is also considered to be the first case of multiple murder in the United States. The story of his crime and execution remains fodder for a horror film.

Barnett Davenport was born on October 26, 1760, in New Milford, where his father worked at an iron furnace. He never attended church or school and in a legal document was called "disrespectful, irascible, lewd, profane, dissolute and completely ungovernable." He was furthermore known as a thief, shirker of duty, liar, cheat and a schemer. By fifteen years old, he had committed the crimes of swearing, stealing, breaking and entering and horse thievery. His parents farmed him out to work for other families, all of whom sent him back because of his behavior. When fourteen or fifteen, Davenport was sent to Upstate New York to work for a farmer named Stillwater; the youth fantasized about killing Stillwater, and this—along with fears that he would be imprisoned for life—caused him, in 1776, to join the Continental army.

He enlisted as "Barnard Davenport," perhaps because of pending charges against him. He served at Fort Ticonderoga and Saratoga, braved the winter with George Washington at Valley Forge and fought at the battle of Monmouth, New Jersey. Assigned to General John Patterson's command, Davenport asked for a day's leave to see his family when that force was in Woodbury. He never returned, instead taking the place of another in the local militia for payment. He deserted from this command as well and returned to Litchfield County, where the Mallory family of Washington took him in.

Caleb Mallory was born in New Milford in 1712 and became a metalsmith and father of four. He was also a real estate speculator, especially in the area that would become New Preston. By 1748, he owned twelve properties, including the New Preston waterfall. In 1762, he purchased a mill near the current intersections of Routes 47 and 109, where he operated a mill and blacksmith shop and built a home. In need of workers, Mallory took in the nineteen-year-old Revolutionary War veteran when Davenport appeared at his door.

In 1780, the Mallory home included Caleb; his wife, Jane; their daughter, Miriam; their daughter-in-law; three granddaughters; and Davenport. The Mallory family lived upstairs in two bedrooms, while Davenport likely slept in the kitchen, as his responsibilities probably included stoking the fire.

On February 3, Miriam left for work, and at Davenport's urging, the Mallorys' daughter-in-law went off to visit friends. The boarder wasted no time in striking. Caleb and Jane were sharing a bedroom with their eldest granddaughter, who was in the bed with her grandmother. The other granddaughters were across the hall. At some point after midnight, Davenport grabbed a swingle—a flat wooden tool used for beating flax—and proceeded to go upstairs and club Caleb Mallory, who screamed, raised his hands and was clubbed again. Jane awoke and began shrieking, at which point she was clubbed. Caleb, covered in blood, began screaming, "Who are you? What do you want? Why are you doing this?" Davenport beat him until the swingle broke, when he grabbed a musket and beat the couple with that. When the granddaughter screamed, "What is wrong with grandmother?" Davenport struck her with the musket. Davenport, in a confession, reflected on this act:

> *The child, in bed with its grandmother, was seven years and eight months. These cruel blows and piercing cries awoke the tender babe, in shocking surprise, even while I was killing her grandfather; and staring up she asks her dear but wounded grandmother what is the matter. She cried out bitterly; she called for me, or to me by the name the pleasant child used to call me, saying Mr. Nicholas.* [Barnett had worked for Mallory under the pretense that he was his brother, Nicholas Davenport.] *But I continued paying on; feeling no remorse at killing my aged patrons and benefactors. For the child I seemed to feel some small relenting, without remitting in the least my execrable exertions. Probably this child was at this time mortally wounded; for the great and terrible shrieks (which one would think) were enough to pierce the hardest heart, and reach the center of the most obdurate soul.*

Davenport then picked up a pestle and used it to smash open a chest where the Mallorys kept their valuables. When Caleb began stirring, Davenport used the pestle to crush his skull.

Davenport took all of the Mallorys' paper money, their coins and whatever else he could carry. Walking out of the room, he found the other two granddaughters, who, scared by the noises, asked to see their grandparents.

Davenport reported that the elder Mallorys were sick and that the girls needed to go back to bed. He then went downstairs and began setting fires.

In planning the crime, Davenport determined that if he set fire to the house and disappeared into the night, everyone would assume that he had

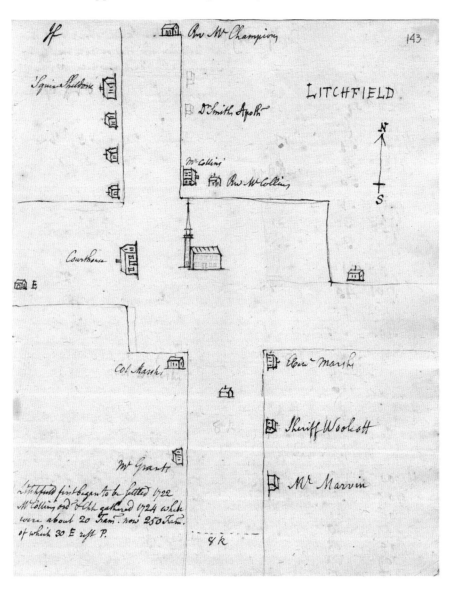

A map of Litchfield, drawn by Ezra Stiles around the time of the Davenport trial. Note the location of the courthouse in the intersection of the town's major roads. *Beinecke Rare Book and Manuscript Library, Yale University.*

also perished in the blaze. Accordingly, he set three separate fires, which soon engulfed the house in flames. It was later determined that the two granddaughters across the hall, told by Davenport to remain in their room, died of smoke and burns, and that Caleb, Jane and the eldest granddaughter were too injured to escape the fire.

The fire did not completely eviscerate the five bodies, so when they were discovered, suspicion immediately turned to Davenport. However, since Barnett had passed himself off as his brother Nicholas, it was for the younger Davenport that posses looked. Sheriff Lynde Lorde arrived on the scene to take charge of the investigation and sent one party to New Milford to the Davenport home and another to follow a set of tracks that led away from the Mallory home. The footprints brought the group to the Blue Swamp, in the Milton area of Litchfield. There, Barnett was hiding out with his brother Nicholas, who remained unaware that he was the focus of the investigation.

On February 7 or 8, Nicholas was arrested. Whether he told of his brother's location is unclear, but Barnett, his escape plans ruined, was captured while he slept in a cave in Cornwall on February 10. On April 25, he was arraigned for five counts of murder as well as arson. He pleaded guilty, and in a trial that may have been presided over by Roger Sherman, a signer of the Declaration of Independence, Davenport was sentenced to thirty-nine lashes while being paraded around the Litchfield green and then to be hanged on the gallows. (It is also possible that Deputy Governor Matthew Griswold, an ex officio judge of the superior court, may have presided; none of the court records are signed.) Nicholas, for his role in providing aid and comfort "against the peace," was sentenced to thirty-nine lashes and to stand on the gallows with a rope around his neck for an hour, to watch his brother hang and to serve ten years of hard labor at Newgate Prison.

Barnett Davenport was hanged on Gallows Hill at noon on May 8, 1780, and his body was left hanging until taken down at 3:00 p.m. Nicholas, meanwhile, was taken to Newgate and was in the prison during a mass escape. With the gates left open and guards searching for the escapees, Nicholas walked out, but becoming confused and lost, he returned to the prison. His sentence was suspended after two years, and he was released with a letter noting his good behavior. He died a pauper in 1800 at the age of thirty-eight.

....

The Mallory Tavern in Barkhamsted, possibly that kept by Thomas Goss. *Library of Congress*.

Two of Litchfield County's four hangings took place in the 1780s. Five years after Barnett Davenport's execution, a perhaps equally gory crime took place in Barkhamsted. Thomas Goss, a native of Brookfield, Massachusetts, and a veteran of the French and Indian War (in which he served as a ranger under the famed Major Robert Rogers), was a fifty-two-year-old farmer and tavern keeper in that town. He had demonstrated some signs of insanity, but what transpired in the early morning hours of February 17, 1785, shocked the county.

His wife had fallen asleep in bed with the couple's three children, including a baby who was nursing. Goss, who had become convinced that his wife was a witch, entered the room with an axe and, with two blows, split open her head. He then smeared her blood over the three children in an attempt to cleanse them from any spells she may have cast on them. Goss then walked to a neighbor's house and calmly reported that he had killed his wife, in accordance with the directive from Exodus 22:18, "Thou shalt not suffer a witch to live."

Even in an era not so far removed from the witch trials, the Goss trial proved outlandish. One historical account reported that Goss "fancies himself beset by the minions of the spirit world and used to speak of goblins harassing him and began calling himself the second Lamb of God." He then claimed to be the brother of Jesus and the son of the woman mentioned in the Book of Revelation, "before whom the dragon stood ready to devour the child."

Ultimately, Goss, like Davenport, gave a confession just prior to his execution. Goss's ramblings in the confession and other material presented at the trial have led Professor Lawrence Goodheart, who has written a history of the death penalty in Connecticut, to conclude, "The evidence indicates that officials hanged a madman." Goss had also been accused of two other murders, one during the French and Indian War and the other of his own child. He began his confession by strongly denying these charges, but, he continued, "That I killed my wife, is indisputable." While Goss confessed to killing her, he used the confession to further his argument that he did so because she was a witch who had been possessed by the devil:

> *Did she say any thing before the fatal blow was given?*
> *Yes, she asked if I designed to kill her; and uttered these words,—O Belzebub, my master, have mercy on me.*
> *Do you remember any other occurrences of that unhappy night?*
> *Yes; the holy angels have convinced me that I got up and lay down in bed five or six times previous to the murder, dressing and undressing myself as often…*
> *Had you any thought of murdering the infant in bed with her?*
> *The devil and I were at strife about it.—He endeavoured to urge me to it; but the angels commanded the contrary, and I laid it carefully away…*
> *Was it justifiable, taking into consideration every circumstance, to kill your wife?*
> *To kill in self-defence is justifiable—she had frequently threatened my life—and often when sitting at table.—Was it not just in Moses to kill the Egyptian, and bury him in the sand?—He acted under the immediate influence of his divine Master—you, from a spirit of malevolence, created by jealousy.—You are indeed mistaken,—I was surrounded with holy angels when I laid violent hands on my wife.*

The Goss trial demonstrated that Connecticut had come a long way from the witch trials of the seventeenth century, as few, if any, were impressed by the religious tones of the confession. While the court found Goss to be *non compos mentis*, this was not enough in 1785 to prevent the execution of a convict. Rather, Goss's execution was set for November 7. When his attorney told Goss he would file an appeal, the condemned told him not to bother, that as the son of God, he could not be hanged. The night before the execution, Goss slept well and even took a nap on the day of the hanging before he ate a hearty dinner. On his way to the gallows, he told Sheriff Lynde Lorde that he could not hang him, that his heavenly father would intercede and if an attempt was made he would be freed and in retaliation thirty thousand men older than fifteen would be instantly killed. On his way to the gallows, he reasserted these beliefs and took a chew of tobacco. He mounted the gallows, had his head put into the noose and dropped. As Goodheart has written, the claims of divine intervention were prophecies "that the sheriff soon disabused."

....

Jacob, Davenport and Goss were all executed while Connecticut used the short-drop gallows. This form of capital punishment involved a short rope, which killed the condemned through strangulation. This was a particularly brutal death, as the convict's face would become engorged, his tongue stuck out, his eyes popped from the sockets and his limbs flailed wildly. Often the noose hung from a tree, in which case it would be placed around the neck of a prisoner standing on a ladder. When the time came, the ladder would be kicked out from under him. Sometimes a gallows would be erected, and the prisoner would stand in the back of a cart with the noose around his neck. At the appointed hour, the oxen would be driven off, taking the cart with them but leaving the prisoner to hang from the gallows.

By the mid-nineteenth century, reform movements led to demands for a more humane method of execution. An Irish doctor, Samuel Haughton, conducted scientific inquiries into the matter and developed a method of hanging using a longer rope, often called the long drop. A noose, at the end of a rope approximately six feet in length, was placed around the neck of a prisoner standing on the trap door of a platform. When the trap was sprung, the prisoner would fall—it took less than half a second—and the force of the drop broke the neck of the condemned, killing him instantly.

....

This was the method of execution that awaited Andrew Borjesson, the last man executed in Litchfield County and the only execution in the county carried out by the state government that did not take place on Gallows Hill.

Borjesson was born in Sweden in 1858. At some point in the 1880s, he immigrated to America but early in 1890 returned to Sweden to

A Revolutionary War–era cartoon, depicting a short gallows in the background. *Library of Congress*.

bring his brother to the New World. While there, he also agreed to bring twenty-one-year-old Emma Anderson with him, but only on the promise that she would marry him once in America. In fact, while in Hamburg, Germany, Anderson told Borjesson that she didn't want to marry him, at which point the latter threatened to leave her there until she once again agreed.

A sketch of Andrew Borjesson, likely from the time of his trial. *Collection of the Litchfield Historical Society, Litchfield, Connecticut.*

The three passed through Ellis Island before Anderson became a boarder with the Homer Buckingham family in Northville for whom she was the housekeeper, and Borjesson lived with S.A. Anderson of Kent. At some point in July 1890, Borjesson pressed Emma to marry him, and she flatly refused. S.A. Anderson recalled that Borjesson "had a bad spell when with me, threw himself on the ground, tore his hair, wrung his hands and cried. [He was] silent for a few days after."

Buckingham later testified that Borjesson visited Emma twice a week until July 13. On that day, Borjesson and his brother arrived drunk, and when Emma stated that she didn't wish to see them, Buckingham insisted they leave, going so far as to take Andrew by the collar and drag him out—twice. But Borjesson returned again that evening, telling Mrs. Buckingham that Emma "does not seem satisfied with me. If I had my money I should be satisfied." He demanded payment for the twenty-seven dollars he paid for Emma's ticket and another forty-seven dollars for a ring, shawl and satchel he had given her. His brother became physical with Emma, grabbing and shaking her. Buckingham gave him thirty dollars and as many of the items as he could find.

This seems to have satisfied Borjesson only for a short time. August 1 was a very warm night, with a heavy rain shower. Borjesson had been out drinking—"fired up with rum," as he later told a friend. Concerned that "somebody else would take care of the girl," Borjesson determined to go to the Buckinghams' to see Emma. In his confession, he recalled:

> When I got there I looked for a ladder to get up to the girls room. I could not find any…I finally found a pile of boards on the side of the road so I took one of those big heavy planks to crawl up on the roof. I went through the window and the girl was sleeping. She was scared and woke up and asked who that was? I told her Andrew…I asked her why she did not come down to see me as I told her in my letter. Emma said that the folks would not let her go, that was all she would say. I backed down to the stand that stood on the corner side of the room and Emma said you had better go before the folks get up downstairs. Those were her last words. I was all fixed and struck her with my hand, the girl jumped out of bed and slapped me with her left hand on my shoulder. I struck her three or four times with the knife and then jumped out on the roof.

Medical examiners would later determine that Emma had been slashed a total of eight times, three of which were mortal: a six-and-a-half-inch wound from ear to ear that severed her spinal cord, another that cut her jugular vein and a third in the breast. Nearly all of her blood was on the bed.

Emma's screams woke Homer Buckingham. It was 3:30 a.m. He raced outside, where he saw a figure on his roof. Borjesson began screaming, "I am here, I am here, I tell you I am here," and then jumped off the roof. Mrs. Buckingham, meanwhile, ran to Emma's room, where her feet were quickly covered in blood. Homer Buckingham entered the room, went to Emma's body and said, "He has killed her!"

Borjesson, meanwhile, ran across the Buckinghams' yard and jumped into a brook in the woods. It was here, according to his employer, that Borjesson began to feel sorry about what he had done. He remained in the brook for the next several hours. As word spread about the murder, a posse formed to search for the perpetrator. It didn't take them long to find him in the brook. George Barnum, one of the men in pursuit of Borjesson, said the accused remarked, "I hain't done anything," when confronted by the posse. When asked why all his clothes were bloody, Borjesson was silent.

Borjesson's lawyer employed an interesting—and typical of the time period—defense. Borjesson suffered from epilepsy, which at the time was believed to produce moral irresponsibility. Dr. William Wild of Danbury, who had been a practicing physician for twenty years, testified for the defense that "epileptic attacks would weaken a man's mind and nervous system. Supposing that a man were jilted by the woman he loves, whom he had brought from Sweden expecting to marry and himself subject to epilepsy, the effect would be disastrous." Wild stated that he had examined Emma's wounds and determined that they could only have been inflicted by someone not of a sound mind. He concluded that "when an epileptic commits a crime and afterwards uses violent gestures and loud words they are an indication of insanity." Even friends and physicians from Sweden sent certificates testifying to Borjesson's good character.

Devastating testimony was offered for the prosecution, however, by Dr. H.P. Stearns of the Hartford Insane Asylum. Having examined Borjesson, Stearns "saw no indications of loss of memory, or impairment of faculties. His replies seemed intelligent. I have detected nothing to indicate that he is irresponsible…A great many people suffer from occasional attacks of epilepsy whose minds are not perceptibly affected." It was, therefore, no surprise that a jury of twelve men from across the county convicted Borjesson of murder and sentenced him to hang on January 29, 1892.

As his execution neared, Borjesson sat for an interview with a reporter from the *Litchfield Enquirer*; he reflected, "I have been in this jail 18 months and there has not been a day or night passed ever since I came here without my thinking of this crime and Emma Anderson…I ought to have kept away from the house and let the girl alone, I believe my mind was good but some bad feeling in my heart, and awful temptation and horror was in my body. But no one told me to do it that is my own fault."

Borjesson's execution became a major event in the county. As a newspaper reported, "it was the first execution at Litchfield in more than a century and few were willing to forego such an occasion." Thousands of people assembled on the town green, opposite the jail, where a temporary structure had been assembled to house the gallows to "shut out the view of the execution from the upper windows of the dwelling houses which are near by." The gallows themselves were designed by a well-known doctor in New Haven who had conducted a study of capital punishment. A contractor from New Milford named Peck assembled the gallows, which had already been used to execute six men, including Jacob Scheel of New Canaan the previous April. (In fact, the rope, cap and strap used for Borjesson were all the same as those used for Scheel.)

The night before the execution, Borjesson met with the Reverend Fritz Erickson, reading a Swedish Bible, until 11:45 p.m. On January 29, the condemned rose at 5:00 a.m., was shaved by the jail barber and put on a black suit. Offered a breakfast of coffee, beefsteak, bread, butter and cake, he declared he wasn't hungry but then accepted the coffee and cake. At some point, Borjesson's lawyer discovered a technicality that could stop the execution—the judge who signed the death warrant was not the same as the one who presided over the trial—but at 10:30 a.m. a properly signed warrant was read to Borjesson, who had just said farewell to his brother.

A procession including the sheriff, jailer, deputy sheriffs, state prison officials and Reverend Erickson led Borjesson to the gallows, where he mounted the steps unassisted. The sheriff removed his hat, which was the signal for the crowd inside the temporary building—estimated at 250, almost all without credentials—to be silent so the minister could pray. Borjesson followed this with some "quiet and indistinct comments" ending with "that is all." Deputy Sheriff Richmond placed the noose around his neck while Deputy Sheriff Marble pulled the cap over his head. The trap was sprung, and six minutes after the party entered the room, it was all over.

While pulse readings could still be felt for eleven minutes and Borjesson's shoulders convulsed once or twice, these were attributed to muscular twitchings and not an effort to breathe. The jail physician, C.O. Beldon of Litchfield, declared that death was instantaneous and painless. The newspaper's observer stated that "every detail of the execution was carried out without delay or painful mistake whatever."

Outside the jail was a different story. "The Town Green was packed with a seething mass of humanity from end to end," the *Litchfield Enquirer* reported. "There was great fear lest a human stampede erupt. When the black flag of death was hoisted above the jail a great cheer burst forth from the crowd." The only criticism of the execution, the paper continued, "is that an unnecessarily large number view the scene, many of whom were more or less intoxicated."

· ·

Small towns like most of those in Litchfield County could rarely count on law enforcement officials to prevent crime. Beyond a constable or justice of the peace, the towns lacked any type of law enforcement. Therefore, it sometimes fell to residents to uphold the law. In Morris, for example, a vigilance society was established in 1871 for, according to the *Litchfield Enquirer*, "the detection of theft or other crimes too prevalent in this vicinity." Still, such citizen watchdog groups could not stop all crime, and on July 22, 1886, an itinerant farmhand killed fifteen-year-old Mattie Randall of Morris. Randall, the secretary of the town's Society of Christian Endeavor, was the first murder victim in the town's history.

A funeral was held at the Randall farmhouse on July 24, and a long train of mourners made their way over twenty miles to bury the young girl in the Bridgewater Cemetery. That day and the next, large numbers of men—over five hundred in all—turned out to search for the perpetrator of the crime. They came from Morris, Litchfield, Watertown, Torrington, Bethlehem, Woodbury and Thomaston and included over one hundred men from Thomaston's Plume and Atwood shop alone. The Randall farm was turned into a headquarters, and women from the surrounding countryside flooded the home with food for the posse members. News that pounds of meat, cheese and cakes were missing from the nearby farm of George Johnson gave the men hope that the murderer was still in the area.

Many of the members of the posse were Civil War veterans and carried with them their rifles, revolvers and swords. They organized themselves in a line of battle, with skirmishers thrown off their flanks, and headed into the woods. A group of two boys and a young man, however, went off perpendicular to the main body, and passing by the Johnson farm, they crossed a three-acre meadow. On the far side of the meadow, dangling from a dead chestnut tree, was the dead body of Charles Lockwood. The boys rushed back to the Randall farm with news of their discovery, and as the *New York Times* reported, "Old and young were swept up in the rush over rocks and fences. Old veterans said it looked more like the charge of a rebel brigade than anything else." Over 2,500 people assembled in the meadow, and a great cheer went up when it was determined that Lockwood was indeed the thief and murderer. Soon, however, the crowd took up the question of whether Lockwood had committed suicide or been lynched by residents eager for justice, a matter that remains unresolved.

······················

Not all crimes in Litchfield County were as serious, and neither were their punishments. It is reported that the men who sat on cracker barrels in front of the Milton General Store had their own way of dealing with criminals. Apparently, a large number of egg pilferers came into the store, and one in particular would secretly put the eggs in his pocket. The regulars would then call the man over to sit with them and then slide up close to break the eggs. If the man declined their offer of a seat, they would stumble and fall against him with what the *Chronicles of Milton* called "predictable results." Either way, justice was served.

4
TEMPERANCE AND INTEMPERANCE

In May 1789, a group of Litchfield's civic and business leaders assembled to combat what they saw as a growing problem in the town: alcohol. In creating the Litchfield Temperance Society, these thirty-five men were the first in the nation to call for the prohibition of alcohol. Their declaration read:

> So many are the avenues leading to human misery, that it is impossible to guard them all…The immoderate use which the people of this State make of distilled spirits, is undoubtedly an evil of this kind. It is obvious to every person of the smallest observation that from this pernicious practice follows a train of evils difficult to be enumerated. The morals are corrupted, property is exhausted, and health destroyed, and it is most sincerely to be regretted that from a mistaken idea that distilled spirits are necessary to laboring men, to counteract the influence of heat, and give relief from severe fatigue, that a most valuable class of citizens have been led to contract a habit of such dangerous tendency. Hence arises the inability to pay public taxes, to discharge private debts, and to support and educate families.
> …Whereupon we do hereby associate, and mutually agree, that hereafter we will carry on our business without the use of distilled spirits as an article of refreshment, either for ourselves, or those whom we employ, and that instead thereof, we will serve our workmen with wholesome food, and common, simple drinks of our own production.

While the temperance movement would grow out of the actions of this Litchfield group to become a major political and moral force in American life, what made this 1789 declaration so significant was the pervasiveness of alcohol in early America.

....

Cider was the most popular beverage of the time, as water was often considered unhealthy to drink. Cider was also an important outlet by which farmers could turn a perishable product into a lasting one. Once it was barreled, cider was easy to transport to markets. Recipes for cider were widespread in the nineteenth century, with most farmers having their own favorite blend.

Apples were ground before pressing. These ground apples would be placed in a bucket, underneath a wooden disc attached to a screw. By turning the screw, the disc would exert pressure on the apples, turning them into liquid and pulp. Often the press would double as a cheese press. Some advocated cleaning the press; others recommended using the residue from previous batches to add flavor. While some recipes called for unripe apples, others used rotten apples. Some even called for grass to be mixed with the apples. Cider in the colonial era and the early republic was nearly always hard and, as the alcohol level was quite low, was enjoyed by children and adults alike.

A bucolic depiction of cider making. *Library of Congress*.

Cider making was immensely popular on Litchfield County farms. Records from Torrington indicate that in 1775, the population of 843 people produced approximately 1,500 barrels of cider at twelve to fifteen mills. In 1773 alone, Deacon Whiting and Noah North each made 100 barrels. There were two major cider producers in Morris (then South Farms)—the Harrison family and the Throops. Litchfield County also had 103 distilleries in 1810, many of which made apple beverages of higher alcohol content. By means of comparison, New Haven and Tolland Counties together had 101 distilleries.

One tale from early Torrington relates that a crowd from Litchfield traveled to John Brooker's tavern and, as historian Samuel Orcutt relates, "ordering drinks and other supplies to their full desire, being somewhat inspired by what they received, took the landlord to a third story window and put him out, head foremost, and held him by the heels until he promised to make no charges for their entertainment."

In addition to the popularity of making cider, the production of other forms of alcohol was also widespread. In 1816, every town in the county boasted a distillery, and New Milford alone had twenty-six. There were also 188 retailers in the county who sold alcohol, and under the excise laws of the federal government, these merchants paid a total of $3,760 for the opportunity to do so.

One of these merchants was William Battell, who opened a store in Torringford around 1785. This enterprise became quite successful, as Battell became a dealer in all kinds of agricultural products: grains, beef, pork, eggs, butter, etc. He would buy these goods from local farmers, transport them for resale in Hartford and New Haven and return with the goods typically sold at country stores of the time: material for clothing, medicines, hardware, groceries and shoes. However, one hallmark of Battell's store and many others in the county was the wide assortment of alcohol available. A county history from 1887 recounts:

Such a store was not complete without a choice variety of wines, brandies, and liquors of all kinds, imported and of home manufacture; and this was not all: the people drank liquors by the gallon and barrel, and some of them made themselves drunk, and wallowed in the mire like beasts, as well as at the present day. The familiar pretense that persons did not become intoxicated and stagger in the streets, swear and fight and run horses and carouse, just like drunken men, is too shallow to be repeated by intelligent people. It may go for par a thousand years hence, but not quite yet. It was not a peculiarity of one store nor of one community to sell and use intoxicating drinks, but was the practice of a great portion of both stores and communities throughout the United States before and many years after the year 1800.

Of the popularity of alcohol in early Litchfield County, Alain White wrote, "It was not thought possible for the average workman to keep his health without a very considerable amount of rum or cider to restore the vitality consumed in his physical work; the non-laboring class also assumed that it could not live through a Litchfield winter without a large consumption of stimulants."

Alcohol consumption was common even among members of the clergy. The Reverend Peter Starr, a minister in Warren, left an account book for the more than fifty years he served that congregation. Among his expenses were "one quart of rum, one shilling two pence; one quart of rum, eightpence; one quart of rum, tenpence." Another story held that a Litchfield deacon, on the surface a temperance advocate but rumored to be a secret purveyor of spirits, confronted Stephen Deming of the town, who at one point had been a tavern keeper. "Stephen," the deacon asked, "When you reflect upon your rum-selling days, the widows and orphans you have made and the misery you have caused, how do you feel?" Deming thought for only a moment before responding, "Deacon, when I think of myself, by myself, I feel like putting my hand upon my mouth and my mouth in the dust and crying unclean, unclean, God be merciful to me a sinner. But, Deacon, when I compare myself with my neighbors I thank God and take courage." Alcohol was a regular part of church life for the congregation as well; many churchgoers constructed sabbaday houses, shacks where they could stay warm and enjoy a meal between the forenoon and afternoon sessions of the Sunday worship. Prior to the morning services, it was typical for the man of the family to stock the sabbaday house with beer and cider.

• •

While the thirty-five signatories to the Litchfield temperance declaration lived in a world rife with the consumption of alcohol, there is evidence to suggest that they were perhaps more influenced by the experiences of one of their neighbors. Jedediah Strong was born in Litchfield in 1738 and attended Yale, the second native of the town to go to college. While he was

A Litchfield tavern sign. *Collection of the Litchfield Historical Society, Litchfield, Connecticut.*

a divinity student, he gave up a potential career in the clergy for one in politics. In this, he was said to have been exceeded only by the Wolcotts in his level of success. Over a twenty-year period, Strong served as a member of the Connecticut House of Representatives and the Continental Congress, was a judge and state senator, acted as a quartermaster commissary for the Continental army and was a delegate to the state convention that ratified the Constitution. He also spent sixteen years as Litchfield's town clerk and thirteen as a selectman. He left a permanent mark on Litchfield, not only in his political deeds, but also in the milestone he erected on his property, which still stands along Route 202 in front of Litchfield Bancorp.

For all this success, however, Strong fell on hard times. In his history of Litchfield, Alain White has written, "His habit of intoxication gradually grew on him and led him to poverty and degradation." He became a beggar and a ward of the town. Ultimately, perhaps urged on by the show of support by his friends who created the Litchfield Temperance Society, Strong made his own pledge of abstinence, adding an addendum to the group's proclamation that stated:

> *By Necessity and on Principle, in consequence of little experiment and much observation, I have effectually adopted and adhered to the salutary plan herein promised during several months past, and am still resolved to persevere until convinced that any alteration will be productive of some greater good, whereof at present I have no apprehensions whilst Human Nature remains the same.*

Strong's vow appears to have been short lived. He was forced to resign as town clerk and was visited by scandal in 1790 when his wife successfully petitioned the state's general court for a divorce on the grounds of "intemperance" and "personal abuse." When Strong died in 1802, his estate did not even support erecting a stone over his grave.

· · · · · · · · · · · · · · · · · · · ·

A similar fate befell John Allen, one of the signers of the 1789 pact. Allen—at six foot, six inches and three hundred pounds—was certainly one of the more recognizable figures in town. Allen was a law student of Tapping Reeve who stayed in Litchfield to practice. He was described as "ardent, generous and hearty" and was also highly successful, serving as a United States congressman and living in a fine home on North Street. However, in his last years, Allen, as Alain White has written, "yielded to intemperate habits" and lost his wealth and his business, dying at a farmhouse on the outskirts of town.

Lyman Beecher, Congregational minister in Litchfield from 1810 to 1826. *Library of Congress.*

It has been suggested that Allen's plight had a great impact on Reverend Lyman Beecher. Beecher—who today is probably better known for his children Catherine, Harriet, Henry Ward and Isabella than for his ministry—was one of the leading theologians of the early nineteenth century. He was already nationally prominent when he came to Litchfield's Congregational Church in 1810. From that pulpit he delivered his *Six Sermons on Intemperance* in 1814. Beecher warned his congregation—and a national audience—that alcohol "exhibits its woes and sorrows, contentions and babblings, and wounds and redness of eyes; its smiling

SIX SERMONS

ON

INTEMPERANCE.*

SERMON I.

NATURE AND OCCASIONS OF INTEMPERANCE.

"Who hath woe? who hath sorrow? who hath contentions? who hath babbling? who hath wounds without cause? who hath redness of eyes?

"They that tarry long at the wine; they that go to seek mixed wine.

"Look not thou upon the wine when it is red, when it giveth his col or in the cup, when it moveth itself aright. At the last it biteth like a serpent, and stingeth like an adder. Thine eyes shall behold strange women, and thy heart shall utter perverse things. Yea, thou shalt be as he that lieth down in the midst of the sea, or as he that lieth upon the top of a mast. They have stricken me, shalt thou say, and I was not sick; they have beaten me, and I felt it not: when shall I awake? I will seek it yet again." Proverbs 23 : 29–35.

THIS is a glowing description of the sin of intemperance. No pencil but that of inspiration could

* When the following discourses were written, alcohol in the form of ardent spirits, so called at that day, was the most common intoxicating beverage in use. But as the poison in every form is the same, and the effect the same, the argument against this form applies alike to every form. I have therefore made no change in the language.

Beecher's famed 1814 sermon on intemperance. *Collection of the Litchfield Historical Society, Litchfield, Connecticut.*

deceptions in the beginning, and serpent-bite in the end; the helplessness of its victims, like one cast out upon the deep; the danger of destruction, like that of one who sleeps upon the top of a mast; the unavailing lamentations of the captive, and the giving up of hope and effort."

Beecher was among the leading figures of the Second Great Awakening, a series of religious revivals that swept the country in the early nineteenth century. The moral zeal unleashed by these revivals manifested itself in numerous reform movements. Among these were calls for public education, prison reform, better care for the mentally ill, women's suffrage, abolitionism and temperance. Within ten years of Beecher's sermons, there were five thousand local and state temperance societies in the United States. As the movement was born in Litchfield County, it is not surprising that it was particularly powerful among the hills of northwestern Connecticut. In 1829, over three hundred men, women and children in Norfolk joined the Norfolk Temperance Society and pledged to "abstain from the use of distilled spirits, except as a medicine in case of bodily hurt or sickness" and further promised not to "allow the use of them in our families, nor provide them for the entertainment of our friends, or for persons in our employment, and in all suitable ways we discountenance the use of them in the community." Membership in such societies became a badge of honor among reputable men of the county; typical was the praise offered for Edward Manchester of Winsted, who was, in the words of the county history, "a strong temperance man from youth, he has fought rum at every step." Some of these men, like Noah Rogers of Cornwall, even named their daughters Temperance.

The Winsted Temperance Society was also established in 1829, and by 1836 the organization boasted 565 members. The town was also home to the Washington Society, a separate organization dedicated to abolishing alcohol, and the Winsted Total Abstinence Society. Another 374 residents of Salisbury joined that town's branch of the temperance society. More than one hundred deaths in Torrington were attributed to brandy alone, and Reverend Goodman, inspired by Beecher, led that town's temperance movement, which saw an original membership of 39 in 1827 grow to 250 by 1839. John Pierpont, a Litchfield native and Yale-educated attorney and minister (and grandfather of J.P. Morgan) was highly influential in converting people to the temperance movement through his poems, collected in *Cold Water Melodies*, and his play *The Drunkard*. Ultimately, the efforts of these reformers resulted in Connecticut prohibiting the sale of alcohol, effective August 1, 1854.

Ministers were quick to tout the success of the law, which was also known as the Maine Liquor Law as that state was the first to pass such a prohibition in 1851. Within a year of the Connecticut law's passage, a 150-page volume appeared in print, with the title *Results of Prohibition in Connecticut, Being Special Returns Received from Every County as to the Effects of the Maine Liquor Law, Containing Contributions from the Governor and Upward of Fifty Clergymen, Judges, Editors, and Private Citizens.* Typical of these contributions was that of Reverend J. Hiram Champion of Falls Village, who boasted that his town had seen a 500 percent reduction in crime and that "the attendance at my church has been increased by a few persons who were formerly frequenters of our saloons." Champion also described how former rum sellers were becoming industrious members of society. In Litchfield, the Reverend Daniel Brown reported a more modest 50 percent reduction in crime but did add that he had not seen a drunkard on the public roads in three months.

In actuality, temperance laws met with decidedly mixed results. While over three hundred residents of Salisbury took a vow of total temperance, town officials labeled another fifty-seven residents as "habitual drunks." Alcohol was simply too ingrained in society for the law to succeed. Rum was routinely used to get volunteers to work on the construction of public buildings. George Woodruff, who wrote an early history of Litchfield, noted that this was done with Litchfield's meetinghouse as well as the one in Morris. The church society voted that "the overseer shall give two drams of liquor per day to the spectators, one a little before noon, the other a little before night." Even at the church where Beecher had preached his temperance sermons, alcohol was used to ply workers to help with a renovation. An attempt to do the work without alcohol was unsuccessful; Esther Thompson reminisced in a *Waterbury American* article that this was

> *an innovation which did not meet with popular approval. There was a crowd of people around the church cellar, but not enough hands could be found who would lift even the ground timbers into place. Then the strike was seen to be thoroughly on. Dr. William Buel asked William Norton and some other boys to go to his store and bring over a certain box, which the lads found to be very heavy. When the doctor opened it and the company saw a case of liquors, there was plenty of men to handle the largest timbers! The last day when the spire was raised there were two or three Shaker tubs of rum punch set at the east end of East Park with little tin cups near by.*

(Note: this would be the area of the green near where Routes 202 and 118 intersect.)

Connecticut's "Maine Law" was repealed in 1872. Of the law, the *Litchfield Enquirer* editorialized, "We have seen rum-seller after rum-seller brought before juries, their guilt conclusively proved, yet escaping justice by acquittal or disagreement. The old prohibitory Statute of 1854 in this County at least was an utter failure. Of the dozens we have seen tried under the act we can recollect but one conviction."

....

The post–Civil War era saw a renewal of the quest for societal abstinence from alcohol. The driving force in this time period was the Woman's Christian Temperance Union, founded in Ohio in 1873 to create a "sober and pure world." The organization spread rapidly, with branches in Litchfield, Winsted, Thomaston and Morris and regional conventions in Goshen. In May 1878, a Morris newsletter reported that "the Temperance movement throughout the county continues to progress with encouraging strength and rapidity. Morris has been having a very successful series of meetings and the proportion of signers to population in that place is reported to be very large. At last reports the number who had taken the pledge was 209."

Those who took the temperance pledge in this time period were part of the Blue Ribbon Movement, so called for the decoration that adorned their lapels. They succeeded in having the 1854 Maine Law replaced with a "local option," which allowed municipalities to decide for themselves whether they would permit alcohol. In April 1880, the *Litchfield Enquirer* reported, "Rum and justice have never been brought face to face so sharply and with such decisive defeat—indeed such utter rout, demoralization and capture of the liquor interest—as the past week has witnessed." The conviction that week of three men for breaking the Blue Ribbon laws—with $500 fines—led 106 others in the county to settle their cases and pay $2,664.11 in penalties. One man went to prison for his actions.

The leaders of the Blue Ribbon movement even praised Catholics—usually the targets of prohibitionists—for their attempts to rid alcohol from their community. Of St. Mary's Church in Lakeville, established by Irish immigrants in 1875, former governor of the state Alexander H. Holley stated, "The Roman Catholics in this vicinity have erected a beautiful and convenient church edifice at Lakeville within the past eighteen months,

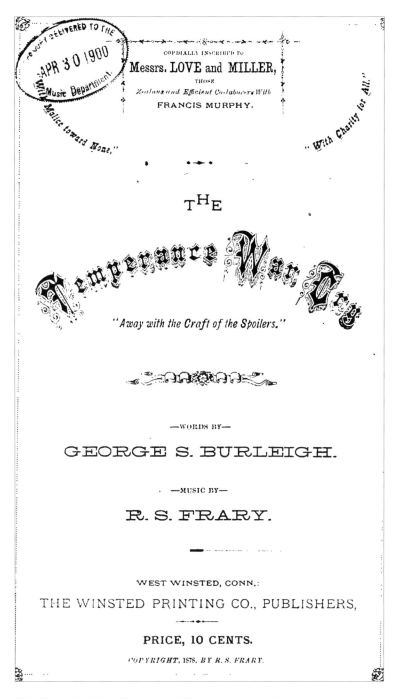

The Winsted Printing Company published anthems for the temperance movement. *Library of Congress.*

which does credit to their taste, and which we hope and trust will have a healthful influence upon all who worship there. The temperance reform which they have instituted has already been productive of good."

....

Supporters of temperance were bolstered by the number of crimes in the county that resulted from alcohol. In one such case in May 1883, Pat Ryan of Morris got "crazy drunk" on cider. ("Crazy drunk," like "jolly drunk" and "beastly drunk" was a medical/legal term for describing a level of intoxication in the days before blood alcohol level could be checked.) In this state, Ryan tried to shoot his wife, who fled to the parsonage. Her husband chased after her with a double-barreled shotgun, a seven-shooter pistol, an additional pistol and two jugs of cider.

The county was also the scene of a 1908 alcohol-fueled murder. On April 12 of that year, Robert Downs of Watertown got into a shoving match with William McLaughlin. McLaughlin was pushed down to the platform of the railroad station, breaking a bottle of whiskey he had in his pocket. Retreating around the side of the station, McLaughlin threw away the broken glass from his pocket and, drawing a pocketknife, raced up behind Downs, severing the latter's carotid artery. Downs was dead within minutes. McLaughlin's attorney, Thomas Ryan of Litchfield, argued that his client's chronic alcoholism rendered him incapable of the deliberation and premeditation needed to prove first-degree murder. The defense was, in part, successful, for after a long deliberation, the jury delivered a verdict of guilty of second-degree murder, and McLaughlin was sent to prison for life.

....

Such stories were not unique to Litchfield County. As the nation became more industrial, the increased frequency of alcohol-related accidents on the job raised an alarm among middle-class Americans. Coupled with this was the belief among middle-class city dwellers that alcohol use among the poor and immigrant classes was making the city a dangerous place to raise children. These fears led to a resurgence of the temperance movement nationwide, with calls for a constitutional amendment banning alcohol.

This 1909 photograph of a roadside drink stand in Salisbury speaks to the pervasiveness of alcohol in the county. *From the F.H. DeMars Collection.*

The proponents of prohibition acted with great political savvy. Advocates first supported the Sixteenth Amendment, which replaced excise taxes on alcohol with personal income tax as a means of funding the federal government. Temperance supporters also worked hard at the state (and later the national) level to achieve women's suffrage, as women were far more likely to support prohibition than men. The final impetus for a nationwide ban on alcohol came with American involvement in World War I. Supporters of prohibition utilized patriotic arguments that wheat was needed more to make bread for the troops than for alcoholic beverages. While the Eighteenth Amendment enacting a nationwide ban on alcohol went into effect on January 16, 1920 (interestingly enough, more than a year after the war ended), it did so without Connecticut's support, as the Nutmeg State and Rhode Island were the only two states to vote against the amendment.

As in most places, Litchfield County's cities and larger towns tended to oppose Prohibition, while it found supporters in the countryside. Still, the relative isolation of areas of the county made enforcement rather difficult.

So did the lack of technology possessed by the county's law enforcement. Without two-way radios, policemen needed to develop working relationships with the proprietors of all-night diners, who would turn on a red light when the barracks needed to reach an officer. Troopers were paid about eighty dollars a month and primarily operated on motorcycle until winter snows forced them into Model T Fords.

William Schatzman, who operated out of the Beacon Falls barracks that covered most of Litchfield County and served for more than forty years as a Connecticut trooper, recalled that judges in the Prohibition era were less concerned about search warrants and probable cause, and therefore troopers could rely more on their instincts. Cars carrying contraband alcohol into the county from New York or Massachusetts could be identified, Schatzman recounted, because they rode so low to the ground. Meanwhile, illegal liquor trucks could be identified when empty; springs were added to the trucks as reinforcement so, when empty, they rode high.

A Mr. MacCurrie, who lived in Thomaston and was interviewed during the Great Depression by representatives of the Works Progress Administration, provided a colorful depiction of attempts by Litchfield County police to enforce Prohibition. MacCurrie remembered one time when he was at a hotel in Thomaston "havin' a nip and a bunch of cops came in to raid it. They was all Thomaston fellas, Charley What'sis-name and Dan Sanger and some more. They searched the place from top to bottom, couldn't find a thing. They was all ready to go out, and Dan says, 'Wait a minute.' He walked in the back room and when he came out he had half a pint. Now by God, you can't tell me he didn't have that half pint when he went in there."

MacCurrie's reminiscences give a Keystone Cops feel to the time period, but even in Litchfield County, enforcing the Prohibition laws was a dangerous undertaking. Thomas J. Wall, born in Torrington in 1879, became one the leading legal figures in the city. A graduate of Yale Law School, he established his own firm (which still exists) in his hometown in 1906 and served in the state legislature and as a real estate developer. From 1917 to 1928, he was the prosecuting attorney in the local police court and was therefore responsible for bringing violators of Prohibition to trial. In March 1925, bootleggers sent anonymous, threatening letters to Attorney Wall and ultimately, on March 18, threw several sticks of dynamite at his house in an assassination attempt. Wall escaped serious injury and in fact made a merciful plea for a reduced punishment at the sentencing of the bombers.

There are, of course, no official numbers on how many bootleggers operated in Litchfield County. There is a Bootlegger Island on Candlewood

Lake, but whether that serviced the county or whether the name is just a vestige of an old legend is unclear. What is certain is that one bootlegger with Torrington connections was beaten, stabbed thirteen times and finally shot to death in 1932. Joseph Curecina lived in Hartford and was murdered in that city on March 12, 1932. Edward Hickey, a Hartford detective, was in Torrington apprehending suspects before Curecina's bronze casket was in the ground. Hickey brought two Torrington men and two Winsted men back to Hartford for questioning. He learned—and the *Hartford Courant* reported—that two associates of Curecina lived in Torrington and that these three men set up an "elaborate still" in the city, independent of other gangs who felt that the three were "cutting in on the alcohol territory ruled over" by Curecina's former associates. Ultimately, the investigation led to Thomas Amico, a Waterbury resident who owed Curecina money. While arrested, Amico was set free when no evidence could be found. And while Florence Curecina, the alleged bootlegger's widow, publicly vowed in the *Courant* that she would "never rest until the slayers of my husband have been brought to justice," there was never a conviction in Joseph's murder.

....

Curecina and the would-be assassins of Attorney Wall serviced what was likely a minority of Litchfield County residents. As unpopular as Prohibition was nationwide (and especially in the more urban areas of Connecticut), temperance enjoyed historic support in Litchfield County. This support was long manifested in Connecticut's last two dry towns, Roxbury and Bridgewater, which voted only in 2010 and 2014 respectively to allow the sale of alcohol.

5

SLAVERY IN LITCHFIELD COUNTY

Few things are as discordant with the institution of slavery as the quaint village greens of Litchfield County. Yet slavery existed in these towns, in some instances for nearly one hundred years. Of slavery, John Dumont, the one-time owner of Sojourner Truth, wrote, "Slavery was the wickedest thing in the world, the greatest curse the earth had ever felt." And while Litchfield County was the native soil to noted abolitionists John Brown and Harriet Beecher Stowe, it was also at one time the home to hundreds of slaves.

Slaves were first brought to Connecticut in 1639, and by 1690 laws had been passed in the colony preventing these slaves from leaving towns without passes. Connecticut residents were empowered to apprehend any who tried. By 1708, slaves were prevented from selling goods without their masters' permission, lest they raise enough money to purchase their freedom. Furthermore, by 1730 a law was on the books directing that any African American who criticized—verbally or in writing—a white resident of the colony would receive forty lashes. As slavery became more institutionalized and the colony grew, the number of slaves in Connecticut increased, with the period of the largest increase in the slave population being between 1700 and 1734.

For its special section "Complicity," an examination into slavery in Connecticut, the *Hartford Courant* analyzed the state's eighteenth-century trade with the West Indies. A study of 144 ships that left New London revealed that iron, the main industrial product of Litchfield County at the time, was one of the major goods traded for slaves that were brought back to Connecticut. Only 7 percent of all captured Africans were brought to North America, so the percentage of slaves that made their way to Connecticut was truly only a tiny fraction of the vast institution of slavery. Still, the number of slaves in Connecticut according to a 1774 colonial census was 5,101. Litchfield County had the lowest number of slaves of any county in the state: 331. Of these, 80 lived in Woodbury (which had not yet been divided into other towns, including Southbury), 62 in Canaan, 37 in Litchfield, 35 in Salisbury, 34 in New Milford and 25 in Sharon. Seven other towns in the county had smaller numbers of slaves.

Slaves literally helped build Litchfield, as John Buell, who with John Marsh received permission to settle the town in 1719, was a slave owner. At his death in 1746, Buell owned approximately two thousand acres and remarkably had 13 children, 101 grandchildren, 247 great-grandchildren and 49 great-great grandchildren. His will, however, listed as his most valuable property two slaves, Martin and Rose.

A similar story took place in New Milford, where Daniel Boardman, who in 1712 moved to the community as its first minister, brought with him his slave Primus Maryland, who was born in the colony with which he shared his name. This should not be surprising; in colonial New England, Congregational ministers were often prominent landowners and could be quite wealthy. As the property of such a man, Primus was likely a well-known figure in town, and both a school district and a large glacial erratic north of what is today Boardman's Bridge were named for the slave.

New Milford, which was home to over 10 percent of the county's colonial slaves, was initially settled as a plantation. When that venture failed, slaves were owned essentially by only the town's wealthiest and most influential residents. Among these were Sherman Boardman, Samuel Bostwick, Nathaniel Taylor, Benjamin Seelye and Partridge Thatcher. Records indicate that Taylor was the owner of a slave also named Nathaniel Taylor, leading historian Michael-John Cavallaro to speculate that the owner was also the slave's father. This practice was widespread on Southern plantations and perhaps in Litchfield County as well.

Excellent record keeping and fine research by Cavallaro provides an interesting glimpse into Litchfield County slavery through the lens of New Milford slave owner Partridge Thatcher. At one point, Thatcher—whose house was recently Adrienne Restaurant on Route 7 north of town—owned ten slaves, five of whom he would free in his lifetime. The owner of a saw- and gristmill, as well as the first attorney in town, Thatcher acquired two of his slaves, Jacob and Dinah, in 1749 when they were eleven and ten, respectively. At that point, they had been in America six weeks. Three years later, the two slaves wed and would have eight children between 1753 and 1770. Thatcher built the slave family a home of their own and educated the parents both in English and trade skills, primarily carpentry for Jacob and household skills for Dinah. When their first daughter, Sybil, sought permission to marry, Thatcher not only gave his permission but granted Sybil her freedom as well, a practice he would extend to most of the family's other children when they reached the age of twenty-five.

The earliest recorded slave in Torrington was Phebe, owned by Joel Thrall, who arrived in the town in 1739 and owned property on the Goshen Road. Phebe is listed as a member of the Congregational church in 1756. In an unusual instance of shared property, three married sisters—Mrs. William Grant, Mrs. Matthew Grant and Mrs. John Whiting (wife of a deacon in the Congregational Church)—co-owned a slave they were given by their father. In 1787, Abijah Holbrook and his two slaves moved to Torrington from Massachusetts to open a mill. Holbrook freed his slaves in 1798.

• •

Manumission of slaves became an increasingly popular activity in Litchfield County as slaves became less vital to the region's economy. Typical of such action was that taken by Mary Roburds of New Milford in 1756, when she wrote into her will: "Mary Roburds, Sen.,…in consideration of the goodwill and respect I have for my Negro servant named Dan…do grant with unto the said Dan Negro his time and freedom after my decease, upon procuring a sufficient bondsman for his security, if need be; and I also give him one bed and covering known by the name of Dan's bed, and one certain horse-colt coming two years old of a bright bay."

The next year, Roburds granted Dan his immediate freedom, without the need for a bond. Bonds may have been used to demonstrate that the freed slave could financially support himself, a practice that would later be state law, or to demonstrate that the individual, in this case Dan, was in fact a freedman and not a runaway.

A similar situation to that of Reverend Boardman in New Milford was found in Litchfield. Judah Champion was minister of Litchfield's Congregational church from 1753 to 1798. This was a prominent position, one that came with a commensurate salary. For Champion, moving to

Litchfield came with a two-thousand-pound bonus, an eight-hundred-pound salary and twenty acres of land. Alain White, in his history of Litchfield, describes how only the most prominent of Litchfield were in a financial position to own slaves. This clearly included Champion, who owned several slaves, including Samson, Kate and Jeph.

Jeph's grave in the East Cemetery indicates that he was a Revolutionary War veteran, but his name does not appear in the Roll of Honor of Litchfield County Revolutionary Soldiers. Jeph's grave is interesting at several levels. It is an impressive stone, inscribed, "Here lies the body of Jeph Africa Servant of the Rev. Judah Champion who Died June the 5th 1793." The text as well as the magnitude of the headstone suggest that it was paid for by the Champion family.

The grave is also notable as the inspiration for an 1838 writing of Nathaniel Hawthorne. In his *American Notebooks*, the author shared

Top: Grave of Jeph Africa, Reverend Champion's slave. The inscription reads: "Here lies the Body of Jeph Africa Servant of the Rev. Judah Champion who Died June the 5th 1793." *Photo by author.*

Left: Judah Champion, minister in Litchfield from 1753 to 1798 and slave owner. *Collection of the Litchfield Historical Society, Litchfield, Connecticut.*

his observations of Litchfield, which include his reflections on Africa's grave (although he incorrectly cites it as the grave of Julia Africa):

> *In Connecticut, and also sometimes in Berkshire, the villages are situated on the most elevated ground that can be found, so that they are visible for miles around. Litchfield is a remarkable instance, occupying a high plain, without the least shelter from the winds, and with almost as wide an expanse of view as from a mountaintop. The streets are very wide, two or three hundred feet, at least, with wide, green margins, and sometimes there is a wide green space between the two road tracks. Nothing can be neater than the churches and houses. The graveyard is on the slope, and at the foot of a swell, filled with old and new gravestones, some of red freestone, some of grey granite, most of them of white marble, and one of cast-iron with an inscription of raised letters…*
>
> *In a remote part of the graveyard, remote from the main body of dead people, I noticed a humble, mossy stone, on which I traced out "To the memory of Julia Africa, servant of Rev." somebody. There were also the half obliterated traces of other graves, without any monuments, in the vicinity of this one. Doubtless the slaves here mingled their dark clay with the earth.*

Cash Africa was a slave of Litchfield's Colonel Ebeneezer Marsh and either willingly followed his master to war or was forcibly brought to the army by Marsh. Cash is listed in the Honor Roll of Litchfield County Revolutionary Soldiers. Traditional accounts say that fighting in the war earned Cash his freedom, but a document in the Connecticut State Library shows that Cash sued Deborah Marsh in 1777 for illegal enslavement. He claimed that he was seized against his will and forced to work for the Marsh family for three years. (The Marshes owned another slave, Nim, who once reportedly killed three deer with a single shot.) A history of Woodbury states that twenty-five slaves from that town joined Cash and Jeph Africa in fighting for the patriot cause in the Revolution. These men, according to that history, "made good soldiers, fighting valiantly for the liberty of the country." They were compensated for their service with their freedom.

••••••••••••••••••••

Even prominent citizens of the county who did not own slaves took steps that increased the strength of the institution of slavery. Roger Sherman, perhaps the most noted politician with connections to the

Roger Sherman (1721–1793), Connecticut congressman and senator. *Library of Congress.*

county, was not a slave owner and long opposed the slave trade. In his political life, however, he supported the Three-Fifths Compromise (which awarded extra representation in Congress and the Electoral College to the slave-owning South), the fugitive slave clause of the Constitution (which federally mandated the return of runaway slaves to their owners) and the Constitution's twenty-year moratorium on banning the importation of slaves. Christopher Collier, one-time Connecticut state historian and a biographer of Sherman, wrote of the deals struck between Sherman and John Rutledge of South Carolina by which the Constitution would be supported so long as the institution of slavery received certain protections; Collier goes so far as to speak of a "Connecticut/South Carolina axis."

Even James Madison wrote that while Sherman spoke of his opposition to the slave trade, he felt that "as the states were now possessed of the right to import slaves, as the public good did not require that it be taken from them, and as it was expedient to have as few objections as possible to the proposed scheme of government, he thought it best to leave the matter as we find it."

....

Historian Gordon Wood has argued that Northern states took seriously the argument in the Declaration of Independence that "all men are created equal." This is reflected in the fact that by 1804, every state north of the Mason-Dixon Line had freed its slaves. These acts of manumission, however, took different forms and usually dragged the process out for decades. Such was the case in Connecticut.

Connecticut did enact a law in 1774 banning the further importation of slaves to the colony. However, in the five years following the Declaration of Independence, the state legislature rejected three attempts to abolish slavery. The major concern was how the African American population of the state would be controlled without slavery. A gradual emancipation law was finally passed in 1784, freeing any person born a slave after that date on his or her twenty-fifth birthday. The law contained "black codes," provisions designed, according to historian Matthew Warshauer, to "restrict social interaction" between whites and blacks. Among these were fines, whippings and seizure of property for actions such as failure to have a pass, vagrancy, violating a 9:00 p.m. curfew, entertaining slaves and selling items without permission.

Even though the legislature, in 1791, lowered the age by which slaves needed to be freed to twenty-one, historian David Menschel captured the impact of the act when he wrote, "The law freed no slave. It did promise eventual freedom to the future born children of slaves…The law reflected the legislature's intent to end the institution of slavery in the state in a way that respected property rights and preserved social order." Furthermore, the law created an incentive for Connecticut residents to sell their slaves to the Deep South, receiving a significant profit instead of simply freeing what they viewed as their property.

....

James Mars, whose autobiography tells us much about slavery in Connecticut.
Connecticut Historical Society.

The vagaries of Connecticut's gradual emancipation laws played out in the story of perhaps the county's best-known slave. James Mars was born in Canaan in 1790 to a slave owned by Reverend Thompson, minister of the town's Congregational church (who also owned Mars's parents, brother and sister). When Thompson decided to move to his wife's native Virginia in the late 1790s, he was legally allowed to bring his slaves with him. This prompted the Mars clan to flee to Norfolk, because there was, James later remembered, "an unpleasant feeling existing between the two towns or the inhabitants of Canaan and Norfolk," and while the people of Canaan would side with their former pastor in searching for the runaways, they would be safe among the people of Norfolk. Thompson first offered freedom to James's parents and sister if they turned over the more valuable sons, but this was refused.

Thus it was that James Mars and his family took to the woods and, with the help of people like a Mr. Cady and Captain Lawrence of Norfolk, eluded Thompson's pursuit until the minister gave up and sold the rights to Mars to a local farmer named Munger, as well as the rights to his brother to a farmer in Salisbury, for one hundred pounds each, approximately $400. Mars later reported that while Munger was "fond of using lash" he grew to think "a good deal of Mr. Munger." Still, a dispute arose over Mars's mistaken belief that the enslaved were to be treated the same as white apprentices and freed at the age of twenty-one and not the age twenty-five. When Mars walked away from Munger, his owner threatened to put James in jail; ultimately, the matter was settled by arbitration, and Mars was allowed to buy his freedom for $90. James's brother Joseph, however, who had been purchased by a Mr. Bingham of Salisbury—also for $100—was kept as a slave until he turned twenty-five.

By the 1830s, Mars had married and was living in Hartford with his wife and two children. He worked in a dry goods store and was a deacon at the Talcott Street Congregational Church; he was also active in both the civil rights and temperance movements. In 1864, he returned to Norfolk and, frustrated to learn that many "did not know slavery was ever allowed in Connecticut," wrote his autobiography, which he sold door to door. He wrote that it was "my privilege and pleasure to help elect the lamented and murdered Lincoln." The autobiography went through six editions. Mars died in 1880.

•••••••••••••••••••••

While Connecticut's slave population fell by half between 1774 and 1790, it remained the highest in New England. Litchfield County's slave population did not fall by half in this time period, even though Southbury, which had a significant number of slaves, was no longer a part of the county. There were 178 slaves in Litchfield County in the nation's first census in 1790. These were primarily the property of families who owned a single slave, most likely a household servant. The largest slaveholder in the county (records from some towns were not disaggregated, thus it is unknown which town he was from) owned seven slaves; one resident of New Milford owned six slaves. There were twenty-one slaves in New Milford, nineteen in Cornwall and eleven in Woodbury.

Litchfield was among the towns where the data was not disaggregated; there is, however, a record of some of the names of Litchfield slave owners. Wills and other probate records show that much of the wealth of the earliest settlers of town was tied up in slaves, and while in the wake of the Revolution most Litchfield families were not in a financial position to own slaves, between 1783 and 1793 growing economic prosperity resulted in the highest number of slaves in the town's history. In his study of residents of Litchfield, George C. Woodruff identified twenty-nine slaves, with their names, owners and dates of birth, in the town between 1777 and 1800. Still, slave ownership remained the purview of the town's wealthiest and most prominent citizens. Among the slave owners in town were the aforementioned Reverend Champion, Julius Deming, Oliver Wolcott (who owned six slaves) and Ephraim Kirby, a prominent soldier and government official whose grandson was the noted Confederate general Edmund Kirby Smith.

A typical Litchfield County slave owner's story is that of Benjamin Tallmadge, a Revolutionary War hero who became a prominent merchant in Litchfield after the war. After getting married and establishing a household in Litchfield, Tallmadge realized he needed domestic help. Thus, he purchased two slaves. Prince was a seven-year-old boy whom Tallmadge purchased from John Shethar for thirty-six pounds on May 19, 1784. Three years later, Tallmadge spent another thirty-six pounds on Jane, a thirteen-year-old girl he bought from Ezra L'Hommedieu. A third slave of Tallmadge, Tom Jackson, was freed at some point and lived with his wife and daughter on Milton Road until after 1857.

In Milton, the Welch family ran a store in a home that still stands at the corner of Milton Road and Potash Road. The store catered to both the ironworkers in the Salisbury area and the stagecoach passengers passing through the village. John Welch received the home from his father as a wedding gift in 1784; the store was in the eastern end of the house. Welch was a great supporter of the Trinity Episcopal Church in Milton, a delegate to the 1818 Connecticut constitutional convention, and the owner of six slaves, who helped make the family enterprises so successful.

The prominent Wolcott family—patriarch Oliver Wolcott Sr. was a signer of the Declaration of Independence—owned numerous slaves, including one named Caesar, who was freed in 1780. Oliver Wolcott Sr. granted Caesar's freedom in a document stating:

An 1813 Gilbert Stuart portrait of Oliver Wolcott Jr. *Collection of the Litchfield Historical Society, Litchfield, Connecticut.*

> *I, Oliver Wolcott, of Litchfield, in the State of Connecticut, in expectation that my negro servant man, Caesar, will, by his industry, be able to obtain a comfortable subsistence for himself, and that he will make a proper use of the freedom which I hereby give him, do discharge, liberate, and set free him, the said Caesar, and do hereby exempt him from any further obligations of servitude to me, by heirs, and from every other person claiming authority over him, by, from, or under me. And that my said servant, whom I now make free, as aforesaid, may be known hereafter by a proper cognomen, I hereby give him the game of Jamus, so that hereafter he is to be known and distinguished by the name of Caesar Jamus.*

The status and position Wolcott felt he had over Caesar is particularly reinforced by the fact that he felt he was in the position to give his ex-slave not only his freedom but also a name.

The Wolcotts freed several slaves but kept them on as servants. In 1789, Oliver Wolcott Jr. wrote to his mother, Laura, expressing his concern about her well-being. Oliver's sister Mariann had married Chauncey Goodrich two months earlier, an event that caused the mother some degree of worry. The son, however, felt "not so much anxiety on that part, as from the multiplied attention which you will give to the family servants, with which you are burdened. I must request that your humanity to them be not so particular as to suffer your health to be impaired on their account. If any measures consistent with property can be taken to prevent an increase of that kind of trouble, it is surely your duty to attempt them."

While it was common for county residents to boast of how well they treated their slaves—the aforementioned history of Woodbury says, "It is true slaves were treated kindly, educated, their religious interests cared for…treated more like children than slaves"—Wolcott's letter clearly indicates a belief that there was a limit to how much masters should care for their servants.

....

It is particularly disturbing to think that in Litchfield—the hometown of Harriet Beecher Stowe, who did so much to illustrate the horrors of the Fugitive Slave Act—other residents hunted down their own escaped slaves. As in the South, Litchfield County's slaves sometimes ran away. The June 7, 1797 issue of the *Litchfield Monitor* advertised for the return of "a mulatto servant Jep, 21 years old, about five feet 7 or 8 inches, understands the trade of Bloomer, will probably seek employment in that field." While it is possible that Jep was an indentured servant or apprentice and not a slave, other advertisements left no doubt. The October 23, 1805 issue of Litchfield's the *Witness* newspaper carried an advertisement posted by John Bird of South Farms, offering a twenty-dollar reward for the return of his "man slave, by name Tom." The slave apparently "ran away on the 21st instant about midnight." Tom was the longtime servant of John's father, Doctor Bird. The advertisement ran for three months, suggesting that Tom was never found.

Sometimes the issue of aiding and abetting runaway slaves landed Litchfield County residents in jail. Jonathan Prindle of Watertown was sued by David Buckingham, who claimed the defendant had persuaded Buckingham's slave Jack Adolphus to run away. Adolphus, twenty years old at the time, still had five years of service due to Buckingham before he would be freed under the state's gradual emancipation law.

....

In the first decade of the nineteenth century, with the international slave trade banned, the cotton gin causing demand for slave labor in the South to soar and the transformation of the Northern economy to an industrial footing, the numbers of slaves in Litchfield County fell dramatically. By 1800, there were only seven slaves left in Litchfield, with the institution forever gone from the town within the next few years. (There were, however, several free African Americans living in the town who had once been slaves.) Goshen and Sharon each still had one slave living within their borders in the 1830 census, a fact that is particularly difficult for a twenty-first-century audience to come to grips with. Finally, in 1848, with approximately only six slaves still residing in the state, the Connecticut Legislature enacted a law declaring that "no person shall hereafter be holden in slavery in this state."

The decision to end slavery, however, did not instantly turn all Litchfield County residents into abolitionists. In 1837, an organizational meeting of a new county abolition society was held in an unheated barn in Torrington. A proslavery mob, its courage "elevated...with New England rum," attacked the members with "blowing horns, yelling and beating on tin pans and kettles" until that had scattered the assembly with "brute force." Like much of the North, it would take time for Litchfield County residents to embrace the abolitionist movement.

6

MILITARY MALFEASANCE

The annals of Litchfield County history contain many examples of military heroism, including the services of county men at the Revolutionary War's Battle of New York, the Second Connecticut Heavy Artillery at the Battle of Cold Harbor in the Civil War and the thousands of county men who served overseas in World War I and World War II. There are also examples of treachery, incompetence and lack of judgment on the part of—and against—Litchfield County men.

· · · · · · · · · · · · · · · · · · · ·

Few military men are as associated with Litchfield County as Ethan Allen, for whom Route 7, traversing the western end of the entire county, is named. Four county towns—Litchfield, Roxbury, Cornwall and Salisbury—claim Allen as their own. The best evidence suggests that Allen was born on what is now Old South Road in Litchfield on January 31, 1738. His grandmother Mercy Allen was a widow who bought a proprietor's share at the town's founding. Mercy reportedly helped build one of the palisades that protected the town from Native American attack and served alongside the men of the town in manning its walls. By the laws of primogeniture of the town, her son Nehemiah stood to inherit the property, but fear of Native American attack drove him away from Litchfield to Stratford, and it was Joseph Allen who received the house and land upon his mother's death.

Joseph married Mary Remembrance Baker of Woodbury in 1735, seven years after inheriting the Litchfield property. Together they had eight children—of whom Ethan was likely the eldest—and cleared forty acres of the seventy-two-acre property, a massive undertaking in that era. They also acquired another five hundred acres of woodlots. However, the Allens, considered "visible saints" in their church because they were direct descendants of the Puritan founders, were unhappy with the religious divide between the "Old Lights" and "New Lights" that was sweeping Litchfield. Therefore, in 1739, Joseph purchased five hundred acres in the new township of Cornwall and convinced fifty other "Old Light" families to follow him there.

While Ethan became a master hunter and lover of books in the town, Cornwall turned out to not be the Eden that the Allens had hoped. The Reverend Joseph Bellamy, Congregational minister in Bethlehem and the head of the Litchfield County Consociation of Churches, opposed all moderation in ministers. And while each town's church held an independent charter, Bellamy's influence was so great that he had, in effect, authority over all hirings and firings. Joseph Allen's choice for minister in Cornwall was simply not enough of a fire-and-brimstone man for Bellamy's taste, leading to Joseph's decision to leave the Congregational Church for Anglicanism. Furthermore, he sent Ethan off to Salisbury to study theology under the Reverend Jonathan Lee in preparation for a career in the ministry. When Joseph Allen died suddenly, Ethan put his ministerial aspirations aside to save the family farm. Life as a farmer was too tame for his free spirit, however, and Ethan was soon back in Salisbury, looking to make his fortune in the iron industry.

The decision to not pursue a career in the ministry was probably a wise one for the rambunctious Allen. During his time in Salisbury, he twice had run-ins with the law. In the first instance, Allen defied a public ban on inoculations by having himself vaccinated against smallpox while in front of the town meetinghouse. When told by selectman Peter Stoddard that he was in violation of a town law, Allen exploded: "By Jesus Christ I wish that I may be bound down in Hell with old Beelzebub a thousand years in the lowest pit of Hell and that every little insipid devil should come along, by and ask the reason of Allen's lying there, if it should be said he made a promise… that he would have satisfaction of Lee and Stoddard and did not fulfill it."

These were fighting words, which called for a duel. Instead, Allen was arrested on charges of breach of peace and blasphemy. Acting as his own attorney, Allen won the case by arguing that he had said, "By Jesus Christ," and therefore did not blaspheme. Still, his behavior had lost him the respect

THE GREEN MOUNTAIN BOYS IN COUNCIL.

Ethan Allen, Litchfield County native, and his Green Mountain Boys planning an action during the Revolutionary War, from an 1858 issue of *Harper's Monthly*. *Library of Congress.*

of town leaders, a loss that was amplified when Allen was arrested for blasphemy a second time in 1771, this time for referring to the colonial governor as a "damned scoundrel." Perhaps tensions between himself and the residents of Salisbury led to his leaving the town to seek opportunities in land speculation in Vermont.

It was as a Vermonter that Allen won his greatest acclaim. Becoming the leader of the militia force known as the Green Mountain Boys, Allen led them to victory at Fort Ticonderoga on May 10, 1775, less than one month after the Revolutionary War opened at Lexington and Concord. The cannons seized at Ticonderoga were essential to George Washington's expulsion of the British from Boston, and Allen became an American hero. While Allen truly suffered for the American cause as a British prisoner of war, he was also voted out as commander by the Green Mountain Boys, who had apparently tired of his arrogance.

When Ethan Allen returned to Vermont in 1778, he found that the state had declared itself an independent republic, and he was named a brigadier general and placed in charge of the state's militia. Vermont was, however, in a precarious state, as it was claimed by New York State, New Hampshire and even Connecticut. Quebec also believed that it owned its southern neighbor.

The Continental Congress debated bringing Vermont into the Union as a state but ultimately tabled the motion, as it didn't want to anger New York, and Vermont refused to set aside claims to towns on the New Hampshire side of the Connecticut River.

It was in this atmosphere that Allen was approached on March 30, 1780, by an unidentified farmer who delivered him a message. It was soon made clear to the general that the farmer was, in fact, an undercover British soldier and that the message was an offer of a generalship in the British army sent by Colonel Beverly Robinson, commander of the King's American Regiment, a unit composed of loyalists. Robinson was acting as an agent for Frederick Haldiman, governor of Quebec, who sought Allen's assistance in delivering Quebec to the crown. This was being done at the same time that Benedict Arnold's treasonous exploits were underway, and, in fact, Robinson was an agent in securing that American's services as well.

Haldiman thought he knew his quarry well. Of Allen, he had written, "I am assured by all [Loyalists spies] that no dependence can be had in him." Furthermore, he felt that Allen's character was "well-known and his followers are a collection of the most abandoned wretches that ever lived, to be bound by no Laws or ties." In short, the governor believed that Allen was not bound to the Americans by any pangs of patriotism, and would—as he had done before—turn away from friends and neighbors for economic opportunity.

Allen sent the messenger back to Robinson without a reply but immediately sat down with his brother Levi and Thomas Chittenden, governor of Vermont, to discuss the matter. Ultimately, they decided to do nothing in the immediacy but rather to use the offer to secure what was best for Vermont. In doing so, historian Charles Jellison has written that Allen and his cohorts left themselves "perilously close to treason."

In his own writings, Allen defended himself by saying that he was simply leading the British on so that Vermont would be protected from enemy raids while he could rally Vermonters to accept the Articles of Confederation and formally join the Americans. Allen, however, only made this defense when his negotiations with the British became a matter of public record. Jellison argues that the evidence is clear that Allen and his brother were determined to deliver Vermont to the British, and Allen himself wrote, "In the time of General Haldiman's command, if Great Britain could have offered Vermont protection, they would readily have yielded up their independence and become a province of Great Britain." And while Allen argued that at the time he was working not for the United States but for an independent

Vermont and therefore his actions could not be treasonous, only Vermonters recognized this independence. The Americans considered Vermont officially part of New York State; even if Allen's defense is accepted, would not turning over an independent Vermont to the British also have been treason?

It is entirely possible that Allen's actions were done with the best interests of Vermont in mind. However, it is also possible that he had other, more personal, motivations. Allen owned significant amounts of land in the disputed areas of Vermont, and American victory in the war would likely mean congressional recognition of New York's claims to Vermont. This would result in Allen forfeiting his claims to those of New Yorkers.

With the end of the war, the United States government set aside the question of Vermont's status, and Allen was content to step out of the limelight to write memoirs and a work of philosophy. When he was approached by followers of the populist rebel Daniel Shays to become the leader of their movement, he declined but effectively offered a place of exile to Shaysites when their revolt collapsed. Allen died in 1789, two years before Vermont became the fourteenth state.

. . . .

Another Revolutionary War hero associated with Litchfield was Benjamin Tallmadge. Born on Long Island in 1754, Tallmadge rightly earned the nickname "George Washington's commando" for his exploits as an intelligence officer during the war. He was the organizer of, and a major player in, the Culper Ring, an espionage operation that provided Washington with invaluable information. The group brought information out of British-occupied New York and signaled messages across the Long Island Sound to Washington's army. Among their discoveries were the British plans to attack General Rochambeau's French army in Newport, Rhode Island, the treason of Benedict Arnold and a British plan to counterfeit American money. The exploits of the Culper Ring have formed the basis for several books, as well as the AMC television series *TURN*.

Tallmadge traveled through Litchfield in the course of his military service, deciding to settle in the town after the war. He built an impressive house on North Street, commensurate with his wealth, and became one of the town's leading citizens. While he was a successful merchant in the postwar period, that wealth was based on money made during the war by means that, while legal in the 1780s, would be questioned today.

COL. BENJAMIN TALLMADGE.

Benjamin Tallmadge, Revolutionary War hero, privateer and land speculator. *Library of Congress.*

Operating as a commando, Tallmadge seized two British ships, the *Sulham* and the *Three Brothers*, and as their captor personally took a share of the spoils. While this was perfectly legal, Tallmadge also felt justified because as an officer he had to pay for his own uniform and food, and his pay from the Continental Congress was perpetually late. These operations seemed to have inspired Tallmadge to think on a grander scale, for soon after, he wrote to his friend and business colleague Jeremiah Wadsworth, "Some of us young lads who were just beginning in the world are spending our time and exposing our lives and health for but the paltry consideration in the pecuniary way. I have for some time been determined to try my luck at Privateering."

The infant American republic was in no position to challenge British control of the high seas with a traditional navy. Therefore, the Americans pinned their hopes for naval successes on privateers, individually owned and outfitted vessels that preyed on enemy shipping. These privateers were granted Letters of Marque and Reprisal by the government to legally distinguish them from pirates. Privateers that captured an enemy ship would bring the vessel to an admiralty court, which would determine if the seizure was legal. If it was, the proceeds from the sale of the ship would be divided between the privateering vessel's owners and crew. Approximately eight hundred American vessels were commissioned as privateers during the war, and they are credited with capturing or destroying six hundred British vessels.

Tallmadge and two other members of his regiment sent $1,000 to Wadsworth to invest in a privateer. Wadsworth organized groups that bought shares in several different privateers. This was done to minimize the risk, much in the way that mutual funds operate today. Tallmadge's group proved immediately and extraordinarily successful, as one of their ships, the *General Putnam*, captured six British vessels. In May 1778, Tallmadge brought some of the men of his command into his investments, having them appoint him as their "lawful attorney." These investments turned sour, as five of this new group's ships were captured by the British. Tallmadge repeatedly expressed his regrets about these ventures and his desires to get out of the business, but he continued to invest in ships until he scored a major return on his investment with the capture of the British ship *Jay* in 1781.

Tallmadge used both the proceeds of his privateering investments as well as the captured materiel itself to move into new business ventures. His brother John Tallmadge ran a store in Bethlehem, which Benjamin and his partner Miles Beach purchased and moved to Litchfield under the name of Benjamin Tallmadge & Company. They advertised the store under the slogan of "Best of European, East or West India Goods" and stocked its shelves with items captured from British ships.

Tallmadge also used proceeds from his privateering operations to establish a business supplying soldiers with their basic necessities, and he was particularly successful in winning contracts to outfit French armies operating in America. In the course of these business dealings, Tallmadge was caught passing along counterfeit notes drawn on a French bank, but it appears that he was as much a victim of this crime as he was a perpetrator, having unknowingly accepted the paper money from Captain Simont de Valcourt.

In March 1780, Tallmadge learned of a plan by the Connecticut legislature to pay off at full value the paper money that had been issued in 1777. These ten-pound notes had depreciated greatly over the intervening years, and the state hoped to replace them with a more stable currency. With this insider knowledge, Tallmadge and business partner Samuel Webb purchased as much of the currency as they could at depreciated rates and then sold them back to the state for full value, a scheme that they repeated with both Massachusetts and Continental currency.

After the war, Tallmadge used the access he had to hard money (gold and silver) through his privateering operations and government contracts to purchase land certificates from the men of his command. Congress knew full well that it would likely be unable to fully pay Continental soldiers for their service in the war or supply them with an adequate pension. Therefore, Congress gave these veterans land in the West as payment for their services. Returning home from years at war, these men quickly learned that cash was of a greater need than land hundreds of miles away. Men like Tallmadge were all too willing to purchase vast amounts of land from these veterans at a fraction of their value, and these land grants were a virtual sure thing for the investor as they provided yields of several hundred percent. These actions, however, presaged the political battles of the early republic in pitting wealthy ex-officers (epitomized by the Society of the Cincinnati, of which Tallmadge was a member) against the poor enlisted men desperate for cash.

. . . .

On more than one occasion, Litchfield County's finest sons have crossed paths with wickedness while in service to our country. This is particularly evident in the tragic story of Frederick Asa Bacon, who was born in Litchfield in 1812. His father attended the Litchfield Law School, and Frederick, his mother and two brothers attended the Litchfield Female Academy. (Approximately 3,000 women attended the Female Academy in its history, while the Bacon brothers were three of the 120 young men who enrolled at the school.) A voyage to England in 1829 sparked an interest in a life at sea, and he joined the United States Navy as a midshipman in 1832. In 1838, while serving as a passed midshipman—one who has passed the examination to be a lieutenant but is waiting for a vacancy at that rank—Bacon was one of two officers named to serve on the USS *Sea Gull*, a schooner that was part of the United States Exploring Expedition (known as the U.S. Ex Ex).

The U.S. Ex Ex was one of several nineteenth-century voyages of discovery sponsored by the United States government. Under the command of Charles Wilkes, this expedition was sent to circumnavigate the globe, chart unexplored waters and attempt to be the first crew to reach Antarctica. Wilkes's primary qualification for the post was not his high seas experience (he had virtually none) or his ability to lead men (another skill he had not yet had the opportunity to demonstrate). Rather, Wilkes was chosen to head up the undertaking because he was an excellent surveyor and hydrographer. As the expedition progressed, Wilkes's relationships with his men worsened, and his command style grew to reflect his own megalomania, so that many believe he served as the model for Herman Melville's Captain Ahab. Regardless, a series of spats and poor decisions instigated by Wilkes cost young Bacon his life.

The squadron set sail on August 18, 1838, but the ships weren't long at sea before their commander began to unravel. Tensions in the navy ran high before the expedition left port, as Wilkes, only a lieutenant, was given

The USS *Sea Gull* in a storm, drawn by U.S. Ex Ex member Alfred Agate. *Naval History and Heritage Command.*

command over several higher ranking officers. Historian Nathaniel Philbrick writes that a "virtual parade" of captains had gone to see President Martin Van Buren, requesting command of the expedition. One officer, Commodore Isaac Chauncey, told the president, "This young lieutenant [Wilkes] did not ask nor would he receive any advice which had been proffered him. No one knew what he was doing." These concerns of senior officers probably led to Secretary of the Navy Mahlon Dickerson's decision to not promote Wilkes to captain, the rank commensurate with command of a squadron. To do so would have necessitated leapfrogging Wilkes over many senior lieutenants and commanders, which would upset the naval hierarchy. Thus, once at sea, Wilkes expressed his uneasiness with his relative low rank by promoting himself to captain, wearing that rank's insignia and having his men address him by that title. He also responded to the issue of his rank by keeping the other lieutenants close to him, as he believed they were likely to disobey his orders, and posting passed midshipmen like Bacon and fellow *Sea Gull* officer James W.E. Reid to command some of the other vessels.

He soon demonstrated his tendency to be a martinet, in one instance subjecting four marines whose enlistments had run out to whippings when they objected to reenlisting. He also valued the scientific experiments of the expedition over the well-being of his men, ordering a detachment to haul equipment up Hawaii's Mauna Loa while his men suffered from altitude sickness and hypothermia, and had the skin scraped off the bottom of their feet when their shoes wore out. Philbrick suggests that Wilkes's lack of sea experience, his inability to get along with officers and his tendency to over discipline his men probably all stemmed from efforts to justify his self-promotion.

Reaching the tip of South America, a passing whale ship picked up what proved to be Frederick Bacon's last letters home. Enormous icebergs—some reportedly as big as the United States Capitol—and huge waves met the *Sea Gull*, and conditions on board became treacherous. The schooner was soon covered with ice and snow, and waves broke over the bow, soaking the men and leading to the formation of icicles on the sails and ropes. One man remembered the "fore sheets were so caked with ice that they were 'the size of a sloop of war's cable.'"

Bacon and the *Sea Gull* performed admirably in the treacherous conditions, and Lieutenant William Reynolds remembered, "I could scarcely believe that all was mechanical, that her nice and regular motion was merely the result of properties bestowed on her by the skillful builder. It seemed much more natural to think that She had a mind, an intellect, a will of her own & that guided by it, she defied the threatening dangers of the Gale." Still, Wilkes should have recognized that the small ship needed more experienced leadership, but he insisted on keeping the command in the hands of the less threatening passed midshipmen.

By mid-April, Wilkes ordered part of the squadron to sail for Valparaiso, Chile, while the *Sea Gull* and its sister schooner *Flying Fish* waited for a supply ship. The *Sea Gull*, one sailor recounted, "tacked and jibed among the fleet" with a "graceful beauty in her motion and appearance that is indescribable, but which to the eye of a Sailor is lovely to behold." When Samuel Knox, commanding the *Flying Fish*, arrived in Valparaiso, he assumed his sister ship would be there. There was, however, no sign of the *Sea Gull*. When after a month the schooner still had not arrived, the officers of the U.S. Ex Ex assumed that it and its crew were lost; Wilkes later speculated that in the gales off Cape Horn, the schooner might have tripped its foremast, which would have ripped up the foredeck and made her unseaworthy. Lieutenant Reynolds of the expedition highlighted Bacon's personal tragedy by remembering, "Poor, poor fellows, what a terrible lot. The two officers were young men of my age, one [Bacon] if he indeed be gone, leaving a wife more youthful than himself and a child that he has never seen."

The loss of their comrades rattled the men of the expedition, who placed the blame squarely on the command structure imposed by Wilkes.

The grave of Frederick Bacon in Litchfield's East Cemetery. *Photo by author*.

Lieutenant Pinckney alleged that all of the officers of the U.S. Ex Ex knew that the schooners, "of all the vessels most likely to distinguish themselves on the Exploring Expedition," and that "the history of the *Flying Fish*'s first Antarctic cruise and the subsequent survey of the mouth of the Columbia by Lieutenant Knox, justify all the hopes which were entertained by those admirable schooners." In short, Wilkes knew that the capabilities and roles of these ships would make their commanders heroes. Instead of placing these ships under the rightful command of lieutenants, Pinckney bemoaned the fact that Wilkes gave them to passed midshipmen: "The obstinacy with which he maintained a decision so injurious to the Lieutenants and so little in accord with his own solemn assurances to be guided, in all appointments, by rank alone, at once annihilated confidence." Even Wilkes eventually recognized the error of his ways, placing Pinckney in charge of the *Flying Fish*, but not without exacting a price, for Pinckney remembered "the mortification which he seemed to suffer from this circumstance, is the sole cause to which I can trace his strange animosity to me during my subsequent service in the squadron."

Captain Charles Wilkes would become embroiled in controversy for his actions during the expedition, and in fact, Lieutenant Robert Pinckney and other members of the crew brought court-martial proceedings against Wilkes for falsifying rank, mistreatment of subordinate officers, loss of a ship and excessive punishment of sailors. Wilkes criticized his accuser by contrasting "the intelligence, attention to duty, and untiring activity of the lamented Reid and Bacon with all that is opposite in the character of Lieutenant Pinkney." The successes of the expedition—the specimens collected became the basis for the Smithsonian Institution—compensated for Wilkes's often maniacal methods, and he was found not guilty of all charges except for excessive punishment of sailors, for which he received a reprimand.

Bacon was remembered by Wilkes as "among the most promising young officers in the squadron." A beautiful marble shaft in Litchfield's East Cemetery commemorates Bacon's brief life and echoes Wilkes's words in praising him as a "highly meritorious and promising young officer."

....

Although he was only a resident of Litchfield County for a short time, the tragic death of Captain Charles McVay at his home in Morris was the result, nearly twenty-five years later, of a malicious attempt on the part of

The USS *Indianapolis* leaving Tinian Island after delivering the atomic bomb. *Naval History and Heritage Command.*

the United States Navy to absolve itself of the blame of the greatest disaster at sea in American history.

Charles Butler McVay III was born into a naval family in Ephrata, Pennsylvania, in 1898. His father commanded a ship in the famed Great White Fleet and then served as an admiral in World War I. Charles McVay III graduated from the United States Naval Academy in 1920. He rose rapidly through the ranks of the navy and, for the bulk of World War II was assigned to Washington, D.C., as the chairman of the Joint Intelligence Committee of the Combined Chiefs of Staff, the highest-ranking Allied intelligence unit. Still, like most sailors, he longed for the sea and, in November 1944, was given command of the USS *Indianapolis*, a Portland-class cruiser with a crew of over 1,300 officers and men and a distinguished combat record.

Due to her reputation, the *Indianapolis* was one of the most popular ships in the United States Navy, the desired assignment for Annapolis graduates and the sons of the politically connected. News organizations fought to get their reporters on board the vessel, as they knew that it would be at the center of the action.

With McVay at the helm, the *Indianapolis* lived up to its reputation, participating in some of the fiercest fighting of the war, twice supporting carrier attacks on the Japanese islands and at the battles of Iwo Jima and Okinawa. There, on March 31, the *Indianapolis* was struck by a bomb dropped by a kamikaze. Severely damaged, and with nine crewmen dead, it limped across the Pacific for repairs and refitting.

While in San Francisco, McVay received orders for the *Indianapolis*'s most important mission. The vessel was chosen to carry half the world's supply of enriched uranium to Tinian Island, where it would be used to create Little Boy, the atomic bomb dropped on Hiroshima. This uranium was encased in a lead box that had been welded to the deck of the admiral's cabin on board the ship. McVay had been ordered to throw the case into the sea if the *Indianapolis* came under attack and was in danger of falling into Japanese hands. This was, of course, unnecessary, and the ship raced, unescorted, across the Pacific, safely arriving at Tinian on July 26.

The final chapter of the *Indianapolis*'s career began when the ship left Tinian for Guam, where it dropped off its many crew members who had completed their tours of duty and took on 400 new recruits. With a complement of 1,196 on board, the vessel headed for the Philippines for training and then on to Okinawa, where it would join the force preparing for an invasion of Japan. It never made it to the Philippines.

What happened next remains at the heart of a naval controversy. Naval authorities at Guam knew that four days before the *Indianapolis* departed, another American vessel had been sunk by a Japanese submarine. Furthermore, the American code-breaking system ULTRA revealed that a Japanese submarine was operating in the path of the *Indianapolis*. None of this information was given to McVay, and when the captain requested the standard destroyer escort, he was denied, as the routing officer at Guam, who was, amazingly, aware of the intelligence, said the precaution was "not necessary." Instead, the only guidance that McVay received was to follow a zigzagging course at his discretion.

July 30, 1945, was McVay's forty-seventh birthday. Leading up to midnight, rough seas with fog and clouds obscured visibility, and McVay gave the order to cease zigzagging. That was a tactic used in good weather, but under lesser conditions, it was unnecessary as it would be too difficult for an enemy submarine to see the ship. However, as the *Indianapolis* maintained its speed of seventeen knots, the weather improved so that conditions would be classified as fair or good. At 12:17 a.m., two torpedoes fired from the Japanese submarine *I-58* slammed into the ship. That ship's commander, Mochitsura Hashimoto, reported the he "waited until [the *Indianapolis*] got close enough to see what it was. When we saw what a big ship it was, I aimed my torpedoes and fired."

Chaos ensued. The first torpedo slammed into the ship's forward starboard, blowing off the front sixty-five feet of the ship. The second explosion was even bigger and struck closer to midship. The first torpedo struck the ship's gas tank, the second the boiler rooms. McVay was thrown out of bed and smelled his ship burning. He immediately left his cabin and, although naked and barefoot, walked to the bridge to assess damage and give the call to abandon ship if necessary. He told the navigator to get out a distress signal and get help, but the radio was "all blown to hell." Within eight minutes, McVay gave the order to abandon ship, but the public address system was also destroyed, and the command had to be passed by word of mouth.

Further complicating conditions for the men was the fact that the explosions on board destroyed several lifeboats and survival kits. Additionally, naval protocol stated that large ships were not reported as arriving in port; it was simply an assumption they would complete their mission. Thus, because few were aware that the *Indianapolis* had not arrived in the Philippines, no help was sent to the imperiled survivors.

The men in the water did think that help was on the way, in the form of a squadron of PT boats that appeared on the horizon. Hope soon turned to terror, however, when sailor Gus Kay heard another man screaming, "No, those are sharks! It's the wake they make!" The sharks attacked, and as Kay remembered, "they pulled guys right out of the water. We thrashed, trying to keep 'em away from us, but they came right into the group…Tore guys' limbs off. The water was bloody." One shark circled McVay's raft so closely that the men tried to fight it off with a paddle. These were whitetip sharks, possibly with some tiger sharks as well, and while they may not have directly killed many sailors, they did drag bodies away. The severe conditions led to photophobia, starvation, hallucination and the peeling off of the men's skin. Several men killed themselves as their plight became truly unbearable.

It was not until three days later, on August 2, that the wreckage of the *Indianapolis* was spotted by an American PV-1 Ventura plane, piloted by Chuck Gwinn. Gwinn immediately dropped a life raft and radio communications and sent an alert to all ships and planes in the area to help with rescue efforts. A PBY Catalina aircraft landed in the open ocean and taxied on the surface, picking up so many survivors—fifty-six, still a record for the most rescues

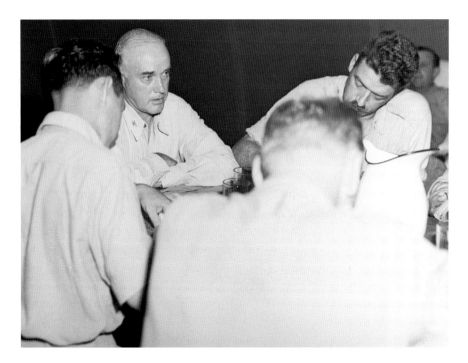

Captain Charles McVay III, with members of the press on Guam after the sinking of the *Indianapolis*. *Naval History and Heritage Command.*

by a plane—that the weight of the men so severely damaged the wings that the plane would never fly again. A naval vessel also arrived on the scene. However, of the 800 men estimated to have survived the initial explosions, only 321 were rescued, and 4 of those men died before reaching port.

The news was kept from the public, and so while military men were in the know—on Tinian Island someone wrote, "This one's for the boys of the *Indianapolis*" on the Little Boy atomic bomb—no word of the ship's fate was released until August 14, and that came only after President Harry Truman announced that the war was over. The *New York Times* labeled the sinking of the ship "one of the darkest pages in our naval history." And with the loss of the ship came demands from the influential families of some of the crew for justice for their sons. Top admirals, including Chester Nimitz and Raymond Spruance, opposed court-martial proceedings against McVay, but the naval authorities in Washington directed that they be held.

Even before the court of inquiry began, McVay told his driver, "You know what? I think they are going to put it to me," and predicted that he would become a scapegoat for his failure to zigzag. Still, it took the navy three and a half months to bring formal charges against McVay, alerting him only four days before the trial that he would be tried for the failure to zigzag and for failing to issue orders to abandon ship in a timely fashion. Adding to the suspicion that the navy was simply blaming McVay to cover its own errors, he was denied his first choice of defense counsel and was not allowed to see the classified information that may have saved the ship in the first place. The first charge was easy to dismiss; the torpedoes had destroyed all of the ship's communication devices. To prove the second charge, the navy brought Hashimoto, the commander of the *I-58*, to Washington to testify, but he instead said that zigzagging would not have made a difference, a claim also supported by an American commander called by the prosecution. Still, McVay was quickly found guilty of failing to zigzag. His sentence was to be dropped one hundred points on the promotions list, a means of effectively ending his naval career. And while McVay returned to duty and was promoted to rear admiral upon his retirement, the stain of his scapegoating by the navy would haunt him for the rest of his days.

By the early 1960s, the retired McVay had married Vivian Smith, a widow and one-time fashion model. The couple moved to Smith's estate in Morris, the Winvian. While the marriage was unhappy, McVay carved out a routine for himself. While Vivian enjoyed the Litchfield social scene, McVay worked with Al Dudley, his gardener and handyman, in repairing fences, tending to the landscaping and maintaining the pool. He enjoyed duck hunting on Bantam Lake and playing bridge at the Sanctum club in Litchfield.

In November 1968, McVay was seventy years old but in fine health; if not for his white hair, he would be confused for a much younger man. On November 6, he woke in his simple bedroom, containing only a twin bed with a Bible on the nightstand and a dresser in which he kept letters from the families of men he had commanded on the *Indianapolis*. Unknown to others, some of these letters were vitriolic in the blame they cast upon him for the ship's loss. "Merry Christmas!" read one. "Our family's holiday would be a lot merrier if you hadn't killed my son." He had received letters like this for over twenty years, the result of the navy's passing the blame on to him. That November afternoon, instead of eating lunch and heading to the Sanctum club, McVay took the .38-caliber pistol off his nightstand, walked out the front door, lay down on the walkway and with his dog at his side, put the gun to his head and pulled the trigger. In his hand was a metal toy soldier he had received as a boy and taken with him around the world, a seeming good luck charm until that day in the Pacific.

The tragedy of the *Indianapolis* has been related many times in popular culture. The character Quint in the movie *Jaws* was a survivor of the ship, and Stacey Keach played McVay in the 1991 movie *Mission of the Shark*. Through all of these portrayals and fifty years of historical analysis of the events that led to the ship's sinking, McVay's conviction stood. However, in 1996, Hunter Scott of Florida undertook a sixth-grade history project on the event, which culminated in a 2000 congressional resolution, signed by President Bill Clinton, absolving McVay of any responsibility for the episode. The next year, the secretary of the navy ordered the captain's record officially cleared of blame.

7

MINISTERIAL MISADVENTURES

There were no great battles fought in Litchfield County, nor were any major battles fought within its borders. But the region has left an indelible mark on American history, and in no area has that mark been more profound than in religion. Given the number of significant religious leaders and fervor of spirit in the county, it is only to be expected that sometimes religion became problematic.

· · · · · · · · · · · · · · · · · · · ·

Abel Wright was one of Kent's original settlers, having bought three shares at the auction of the future town held in Windham in 1737. By 1740, he was the largest property owner in the town, owning a full 50 percent more property than the second largest. Wright was also—as were most of his neighbors—very involved in religion and was an original member of the Kent First Society Church, which later became the Congregational church.

A storekeeper, he sold both local produce—wool, flour, wheat, butter and, of course, cider—and luxuries brought up from New York City on the region's very poor roads. Historian Charles Grant has written that Wright sold hundreds of different items, including multiple types of buckles, garters, fans and gloves. When he died in 1770, he owed 61 pounds to twenty-six different suppliers but was owed 229 pounds by 140 Kent residents.

He was also deeply involved in the civic life of the town. In his first few years in Kent, Wright served as a selectman, a town agent, moderator for town meetings and captain of the militia. In this last capacity, he led the town's troops during King George's War (1740–48), petitioning the town in 1744 to foot the bill for ammunition, noting that "the town of Kent is one of the frontier towns and since there is so much noise of war with the French, we look upon ourselves as much exposed." Wright was a pillar of the town, the kind of man around whom colonial communities were built. The esteem in which Kent residents held Wright, however, quickly disappeared when the shopkeeper ran afoul of religious orthodoxy.

In July 1743, Wright and his wife invited three preachers—James Clement, Benjamin Ferris and Richard Hallet—to their home for a discussion. Also present were Wright's neighbors the Lathams and Rebeccah Alger. Wright had become involved with the "New Light" movement, and the three clergymen were leaders of this branch of Congregationalism, which embraced the revival phenomenon and the idea that the organized church was not the only vehicle for communing with God.

Traditional Congregational authorities, known as Old Lights, were naturally threatened by the New Lights and moved quickly to squash the upstarts. In Kent, this meant that the Wrights and their guests were called before a church meeting on August 4, charged with listening to "notoriously corrupt teachers" and hosting what was called a "disorderly meeting." Wright stood to defend himself but was quickly found guilty of "open contempt of the pastoral authority which Christ hath left to his Church and of unchristian disrespect to Him." As punishment, Wright and the others were denied the right to hear the gospel until they had "made satisfaction"— that is, confessed their sin in front of the congregation.

Wright's accomplices atoned for their sins, but the militia captain was enraged by both the penalty and the role of the Reverend Cyrus Marsh in leading the prosecution. Each side of the dispute began to raise the ante, with Wright first leaving the Congregationalists for the Moravians, who were actively looking to convert the Native Americans in the area. His neighbors the Barnums, who had sympathy for the way Wright was treated by the minister, were furious upon hearing of Wright's involvement with a group that was "frowned on by the government." Wright replied that the Moravians were "the most instructive men he ever saw," good men who taught him "about the merits of Christ and practical, good religion." The storekeeper's defense fizzled when Kent residents reverted to a long-standing belief about the Moravians, articulated best by Gideon Barnum, who proclaimed, "I believe they are papists!" It was this very charge that landed the group in Connecticut in the first place, as the suspicion of Catholicism resulted in the Moravians' expulsion from the New York colony. (Abigail Barnum had a more immediate concern about the Moravians, expressing her belief that they would kill her in her bed!)

Wright went door to door to meet with his neighbors in person and explain his actions. They were shocked at his conversion, calling his beliefs blasphemy, especially since the Congregationalists, like their Puritan ancestors, believed that man lived in a state of grace, while the Moravians, according to historian Grant, believed that "sometimes you are in grace and

Abel Wright's grave in Kent's Good Hill Cemetery. *Photo by author.*

sometimes you are so far out as to be half devil." In the back and forth, more than half of the townsmen sent a petition to the General Assembly requesting that Wright's commission as militia captain be revoked and that the colony's government begin investigating Wright. This convinced Wright to move to Fairfield in 1744.

Within the established religion of Kent, Abel Wright achieved significant wealth and power; when he stepped outside that religion, he was driven from the town. If this is a case that illustrates the grip that religious authority held on colonial life, and the extent to which orthodoxy would go to crush dissidents, it is also worth noting, as historian Grant points out, that this case is unusual in that it was an example of the poorer residents of town inflicting punishment on a wealthy and powerful man. It is also worth noting that those residents were not without forgiveness, for in 1760, Abel Wright returned to Kent, reopened his shop and died there in 1770.

. . . .

Opinions about the intersection of religion and government have changed over the centuries. For twenty-seven years after the ratification of the First Amendment, the Congregational Church continued to be the established church in Connecticut, and for another six years, the town of Salisbury continued to financially support its Congregationalists. Ministers tended not only to their flock's religious needs but provided political guidance and direct governmental leadership as well. The dangers of such interference—and, perhaps, insight into why Connecticut abolished established religion—are exemplified in the case of the Litchfield newspaper the *Witness*.

In August 1805, two aspiring newspapermen, Selleck Osborn and Timothy Ashley, arrived in the county seat and began publishing the *Witness*, an unabashedly partisan newspaper supporting President Thomas Jefferson and his Democratic-Republican Party. In doing so, they brought the political fights of the day into a stronghold of the Federalist Party. Most of Litchfield's leading citizens—including Tapping Reeve, Benjamin Tallmadge and Oliver Wolcott Jr.—were devotees of the party of Alexander Hamilton and John Adams. Counted among this group who viewed Jefferson as "an infidel and reprobate" were two of the town's ministers, Judah Champion and Daniel Huntington.

Huntington served as Champion's assistant minister and on one occasion gave a particularly political sermon, which Champion followed with a prayer that began asking for blessings upon "thy servant the President of the United

States [John Adams]," and concluded, "And, O Lord! wilt thou bestow upon the Vice-President [Jefferson] a double portion of Thy grace, for Thou knowest he needs it!" (Until the ratification of the Twelfth Amendment in 1803, the candidate with the most electoral votes became president, and the one with the second most became vice-president, leading to political rivals Adams and Jefferson serving in the same administration.)

Following Jefferson's election in 1800, Huntington's sermons (Champion retired in 1798) became so partisan that some members of the congregation, including Deacon Lewis, left to join the Episcopal Church. (It is worth noting that around this time a dispute over the correct boundary between Litchfield and Washington arose; ultimately, Litchfield decided that Washington could have the land because it was populated with many Episcopalians.) Huntington wanted a full expulsion of the Democrats from the church but settled for a removal of the "watch and fellowship" of the church over its Democratic members.

Enter Selleck Osborn and the *Witness*. The editor took up the banner of defending the town's Democrats by launching a series of attacks—in print—on the town fathers. Osborn was soon after arrested, tried and convicted of libel and, deciding to become a political martyr, refused to pay the fine and was thrown in jail. His partner, Ashley, was jailed as well but was soon freed and took to depicting Osborn's plight in the pages of the newspaper: he was housed in a cell with two prisoners convicted of capital offenses, the air was foul and the cell so dark the prisoner could not see his own hands, friends were forbidden to see Osborn and the journalist's health was failing. While Litchfield's sheriff, John Landon, vigorously denied the charges, Democrats planned a "grand ovation" in honor of Osborn on August 6, 1805.

While the Congregationalist ministers were at the heart of the town's political infighting, Huntington graciously allowed his church to be used for the meeting. However, before the ceremonies began, Reverend Champion walked up the aisle, heading for the altar, but was stopped by Joseph L. Smith, a member of the planning committee. Smith told the minister, "You have no business here, and must go out of the house." In reply, Champion stated that he hoped only to sit and listen and promised not to cause a disruption. Smith told him to leave immediately, or he would have the military—a cavalry detachment from the Springfield Armory was on the scene—remove him.

While Smith denied these charges, Champion later reported that he was "much afflicted at being cast out of the house of God where I had worshipped almost fifty-four years, and could expect to be there but a few days more. These reflections crowded into my mind when ejected and retiring from the place where God's honor had dwelt." Ultimately, the *Witness* reaped extra advertising from the affair, paid Osborn's fine and soon after shut down operations, with the editor moving on to Delaware. The impact on relations between religion and government, however, had been felt.

·······················

If not necessarily wicked, Litchfield's church stove war demonstrated the heated passions that could be aroused by even the simplest of alterations to religious routines.

Litchfield's first Congregational church was built in 1721 and replaced in 1761. While neither of these buildings was heated, individuals often brought in their own foot stoves during the dead of winter, as services often lasted the bulk of the day on Sundays. These services were divided into forenoon and afternoon sessions, with the congregation adjourning to small shacks, known as sabbath day or sabbaday houses built nearby, for a meal during the intermission.

At that time, the Congregational church was located on land now occupied by the town green. It was the cultural and political center—as well as the geographic center—of the town. Perhaps this centrality has something to do with the uproar that transpired in 1816 when a stove was installed in the church.

In later years, an editor of the *Hartford Courant* claimed to be involved in the episode and related that there was "violent opposition" to the "introduction of a stove into the old meetinghouse" when an attempt was made to purchase and erect one. Henry Ward Beecher recalled that "when the heresy was broached…intense excitement…prevailed on Litchfield Hill. The parties were formed—the Stove Party and the Anti-Stove Party." Ultimately, an "Association of Young Men" appealed to the First Ecclesiastical Society that the church "accept a Stove and Pipe" for the church and, furthermore, that the church consult with the association as to where the stove would be placed.

After much discussion, the church society granted approval. On a Saturday afternoon, the stove was installed, and the editor and his friends eagerly took seats in the choir where they could "see the fun." He remembered that it was a warm November day, "in which the sun shone cheerfully and warmly on the old south steps and into the naked windows." The stove sat squarely in the center aisle of the church and instantly drew the attention of those entering the meetinghouse. Deacon Trowbridge, a fierce opponent whose objections had been beaten down, "shook his head" upon feeling the heat

Litchfield's Congregational church, scene of the church stove war. *Collection of the Litchfield Historical Society, Litchfield, Connecticut.*

from the stove and gathered up his coat as he took his position. Noah Stone, a farmer, allowed only the scowl on his face to reflect his displeasure, until the service reached the intermission, when he uttered "his maledictions over his nut-cakes and cheese." Mr. Bunce, a supporter of the stove and editor of a newspaper in town, walked right up to it and happily warmed his hands. It was Mrs. Peck, however, who had the most visible reaction, "fanning herself, and at length apparently swooned away—declaring, when she recovered, that 'the heat of that horrid stove had caused her to faint.'"

The remarkable fact of the episode—and the stuff of modern-day psychology experiments—is that apparently the stove was not lit. When this fact was revealed to the congregation, "we heard no more opposition to the warm stove in the meeting house," attendees finding that the heat made the long services more tolerable.

. . . .

No account of ministerial misdoings would be complete without the saga of Litchfield's native son, Henry Ward Beecher. He was the eighth of Reverend Lyman Beecher's thirteen children, whose intellect led the noted writer and abolitionist Theodore Parker to declare that Lyman was the "father or more brains than any other man in America." Henry, his Litchfield friends remembered, was fond of stacking bales of hay into makeshift pulpits, behind which he would play minister.

After graduating from Amherst College, Henry enrolled at the Lane Theological Seminary outside Cincinnati, where his father served as president. He graduated in 1837, married Eunice Bullard that same year and moved to Lawrenceburg, Indiana, where he became the popular and successful minister of a poor congregation. The need for money led to Henry's accepting an offer from businessman Henry Bowen to become the first pastor of the Plymouth Church in Brooklyn, a position he held for the next forty years. In this capacity, Beecher began preaching the "Gospel of Love," a renunciation of the existence of heaven in favor of a belief that "man was made for enjoyment." If this put him squarely at odds with the more fire and brimstone message of his father, it also made Henry extremely popular on the national lecture circuit and quite wealthy. Henry also increasingly disagreed with Lyman over slavery, with the father being in favor of gradual emancipation while the more radical son—for whom the rifles "Beecher's Bibles" being sent to combat slave owners in Kansas were named—supported immediate emancipation.

Henry Ward Beecher, born in Litchfield in 1813. *Library of Congress*.

Perhaps the abolitionist movement and the Civil War provided both professional and personal focus for Henry, for with the end of the war, his life became increasingly tempestuous. His public support of President Andrew Johnson made him suddenly unpopular with Republicans. Adding to Beecher's stress was the pressure put on him by his publisher to complete the manuscript of his novel, *Norwood*, which was more than a year overdue. In this atmosphere, paralyzed, as his biographer Debby Applegate has written, "by inexperience, insecurity and chronic procrastination," Henry turned to Elizabeth Tilton, wife of his assistant Theodore, for comfort.

With her husband away on a speaking tour, Henry would bring Elizabeth chapters to read, knowing that she wouldn't be critical. Over time, he brought her gifts, toys for her children and pictures of himself, which she locked away so Theodore wouldn't find them. Eventually, Rose Wentworth, the main character of *Norwood*, took on Elizabeth's characteristics.

The rumors of an affair were nothing new for those who knew Beecher well. It was speculated that he had been involved with Chloe Beach, wife of his friend Moses, and had perhaps fathered her daughter Violet. While Theodore Tilton insisted that he was not jealous, Henry's visits become increasingly more disturbing. Theodore said that Elizabeth "regarded Mr. Beecher as though Jesus Christ himself had walked in," and he was soon suffering from insomnia, fighting constantly with Elizabeth and increasingly turning to alcohol. The Beecher/Tilton relationship was allegedly consummated in 1868, when Henry enthralled a crowd at an election rally for Ulysses S. Grant. In her diary, Elizabeth described it as a "Day Memorable." The relationship apparently continued into 1870, and Henry referred to it all as "nest hiding."

At the same time, Henry was increasingly being pulled into the women's rights movement, in which his sister Isabella Beecher Hooker was gaining prominence. These activities brought Isabella into contact with the suffragist leaders, including Elizabeth Cady Stanton and Susan B. Anthony. In what must have been a confused and unforgettable night at the Tilton house, Theodore and Elizabeth separately told the two crusaders the story of Elizabeth's involvement with Henry.

Further pulling Henry into the vortex were the larger philosophical questions swirling about the institution of marriage. Henry performed a wedding for Civil War hero Albert Richardson and Abby McFarland, who had secured a divorce from her husband, Daniel, in order to marry Albert. The wedding was performed with a certain degree of haste, as Albert was dying of a gunshot wound inflicted by Daniel. However, Indiana's divorce laws were not recognized by the State of New York, making Beecher a party to bigamy. To quell the public outcry, Henry reaffirmed his commitment to traditional marriage, stating, "Men must overcome the causes of unhappiness within the household, or else endure them; two hearts are to be shut up, and forbidden to go out until they have adjusted all their differences—and then they will not wish to go out." Adding to his woes was the irrepressible Victoria Woodhull, a former psychic, rumored prostitute and advocate of free love, who in 1872 became the first woman to run for president.

Woodhull's work spreading the free love doctrine was slammed by Beecher, which under normal circumstances would likely have drawn a response from the free-spirited suffragist. That response turned to outright war, however, when Woodhull learned of Beecher's indiscretions from Stanton and published a diatribe in the *New York World*:

> *I advocate free love in its highest purest sense as the only cure for the immorality, the deep damnation by which men corrupt and disfigure God's most holy institution of sexual relation. My judges preach against "free love" openly, and practice it secretly; their outward seeming is fair, inwardly they are full of "dead men's bones and all manner of uncleanness." For example, I know of one man, a public teacher of eminence who lives in concubinage with the wife of another public teacher of almost equal eminence. All three concur in denouncing offenses against morality…I shall make it my business to analyze some of these lives, and will take my chances in the matter of libel suits.*

When this—and appeals from Tilton and Henry Bowen, Beecher's publisher, for the minister to step down—did not achieve satisfaction, Woodhull named names. She first told a group in Boston that Beecher had for years carried on an affair with Elizabeth Tilton, wife of his best friend; that she had heard the story from both Tiltons and Beecher; and that he had at least a dozen mistresses. And when the Plymouth Church had a twenty-fifth-anniversary party for Beecher, Woodhull responded, "Very well, I will make it hotter on earth for Henry Ward Beecher than Hell is below." On October 28, 1872, *Woodhull & Claflin's Weekly* ran a story entitled "The Beecher-Tilton Scandal Case." This listed Isabella as among the sources and sold out within hours, with ten-cent papers soon selling for twenty-five times that amount. And it led to Woodhull's arrest for sending obscenity through the mail.

The Plymouth Church immediately held excommunication hearings against Tilton, at which Elizabeth stated she confessed only because of pressure from her husband and attorneys and then left her husband. And while the charges against Woodhull were dismissed on a technicality, Tilton fired back by dragging Beecher into court on charges of adultery, suing him for $100,000 in damages. The result was a "trial of the century," with a nineteenth-century dream team of attorneys and the irresistible sight of Eunice Beecher at her husband's trial every day. Under direct questioning, Henry was defiant in his denials of everything from "undue familiarity" to "carnal intercourse" but on cross-examination pled a failing memory (which plagued his father's last days) and evaded direct answers over nine hundred times. He spent more than three weeks on the stand. And Elizabeth, so emotionally distraught that she offered a letter in lieu of testifying in person,

The Beecher-Tilton affair tore apart the Beecher family, especially Henry Ward and his youngest sister, Isabella Hooker (front left). *Collection of the Litchfield Historical Society, Litchfield, Connecticut.*

maintained her innocence, stating only that she was "unwilling to reveal the secrets of my married life." After six months of testimony, and more than fifty ballots, the result was a hung jury. With the vote nine to three in favor of Beecher, the matter was not re-adjudicated.

The Plymouth Church reiterated its full support for its famous leader and instead excommunicated Elizabeth for slandering Beecher. He traveled the country, lecturing to huge crowds while rebuilding his financial standing, which had suffered during the years of turmoil. It was Frank Moulton, an old friend of Theodore Tilton, who perhaps best summarized the results of the sordid affair. Speaking of Elizabeth, he said, "She is a religious fanatic, and so long as she believed she was protecting a saint, she could say things that were not true. She is not unlike Mr. Beecher in this respect. She believes in God and the angels, and when she speaks she feels that God is looking right at her." The difference between her and Beecher, he concluded, was that "Mr. Beecher will swear by God and the angels, but knows that God and the angels won't touch him."

EPILOGUE

What is wicked? Is evil a constant, or do perceptions of it change over time? Robin Hood, Bonnie and Clyde and D.B. Cooper have been viewed as criminals by some and heroes by others. Some of the stories presented here would have been considered perfectly normal in their time; the town of Kent's treatment of Abel Wright, for example, while upsetting to our twenty-first-century ideas about separation of church and state, was perfectly normal behavior in the mid-eighteenth century. Perhaps no story so aptly illustrates changing attitudes toward "wicked" behavior as that of the Leatherman.

Between 1856 and 1882, a stranger clad only in leather traveled between the Connecticut River and the Hudson River, from the shore to the Berkshires and even to Canada. Beginning in 1883, he walked the same 365-mile circuit every thirty-four to thirty-six days until his death from cancer in 1889. According to historian Dan DeLuca, the Leatherman visited the Litchfield County towns of New Milford, Bridgewater, Roxbury, Bethlehem, Goshen, Washington, Thomaston, Plymouth, New Hartford, Morris, Litchfield, Torrington, Winchester and Canaan at least once each, while Woodbury, Watertown, Thomaston and Harwinton were regular stops. Caves and rock crevices that he used as shelters are still accessible in Black Rock State Park in Watertown and Thomaston.

The *Litchfield Enquirer* described the Leatherman in 1877: "He has on shoes of leather, and his cap, coat and pants are made of boot legs curiously sewed with leather strings. He asked for something to eat, and he is not

The Leatherman, photographed in Wallingford in the 1880s. *Connecticut Historical Society*.

refused, for all wish to examine his clothes while he is eating. He expresses no thanks for food, and says little except 'yes.' If he would use a razor he would be a good looking man." He would certainly warrant a suspicious glance from a modern passerby.

The *Woodbury Reporter* described a typical experience with the Leatherman:

> *He has a habit for many years of stopping for food at the old homestead of the late Homer Root. It is related to us that not long ago he called there, and the foreign housekeeper spoke to him in her language (we think it was French) and received in reply in the same tongue a small portion of his strange history. He was a native of a foreign country, had met with great trouble and disappointment, and ever since has been a wanderer upon the face of the earth. He rarely refuses food, and never rejects proffered tobacco and cigars. He comes and goes, unmolested, unknown, but a true record of his life would form a tale more interesting than fiction.*

Alexander Gordon Jr. of Woodbury, a tanner himself, was one of the few to befriend the Leatherman. He would oil the sojourner's clothing for him when it became dried up from exposure to the sun.

Rumors swirled over this modern-day pilgrim's identity. Most believed he was French or French Canadian. Some said he was exiled royalty. A common—but disproven—theory held he was Jules Borglay, who, having lost his love and the fortune he made in the leather industry, condemned himself to a lifetime of walking the same circuit.

The poverty and psychological problems faced by many Civil War veterans led to fears about strangers on the roads. In 1875, the *Bristol Press* issued a warning that "tramps are increasing, and with their multiplication, robbery, incendiarism, intimidation, rape and murder in like ratio become more and more common." The paper went so far as to urge citizens to refuse food or shelter to these men and, if necessary, to shoot them. In 1879, both Connecticut and New York passed anti-vagrancy laws, with punishments of up to a year in prison.

However, the Leatherman was exempted from these fears, a fact twenty-first-century residents of the county might find remarkable. In 1884, the *New York Times* wrote, "No one, women or child, fears him, for all know that he is a harmless creature, and tradition at least has it that he never did and never would harm anybody or anything." One Woodbury writer commented, "Even to this day [the Leatherman] is held in awe by the school-children as well as by some of the older people." And potentially unsettling to modern audiences used to news of schools forced to go into lockdowns, some teachers even allowed their best student to take food out to the Leatherman as he passed by.

Legends persist that upon seeing him approach, children would sing an old Mother Goose rhyme:

One misty, moisty morning,
When cloudy was the weather,
I chanced to meet an old man clothed all in leather.
He began to compliment, and I began to grin,
How do you do, and how do you do?
And how do you do again?

Clearly, one generation's wicked was another's object of wonder.

WORKS CONSULTED

Applegate, Debby. *The Most Famous Man in America: The Biography of Henry Ward Beecher*. New York: Doubleday, 2006.

Bailey, Bess, and Merrill Bailey. *The Formative Years: Torrington, 1737–1852*. Torrington, CT: Torrington Historical Society, 1975.

Carley, Rachel. *Litchfield: The Making of a New England Town*. Litchfield, CT: Litchfield Historical Society, 2011.

Cavallaro, Michael-John. *Tales of Old New Milford: Slavery, Crime and Punishment on the Connecticut Frontier*. New Milford, CT: Arkett Publishing, 2011.

Chronicles of Milton: Village Left Behind by Time. Litchfield, CT: Milton Women's Club, 1997.

Collier, Christopher. *Roger Sherman's Connecticut: Yankee Politics and the American Revolution*. Middletown, CT: Wesleyan University Press, 1971.

Cothren, William. *History of Ancient Woodbury, Connecticut from the First Indian Deed in 1659*. Waterbury, CT: Bronson Brothers, 1859.

DeLuca, Dan W. *The Old Leatherman: Historical Accounts of a Connecticut and New York Legend*. Middletown, CT: Wesleyan University Press, 2008.

DeMars, Frank H., and Elliot P. Bronson. *Winsted and the Town of Winchester.* Winsted, CT: Cahill, 1972.

Demos, John. *Entertaining Satan: Witchcraft and the Culture of Early New England.* New York: Oxford University Press, 1982.

Editors of the Hartford Courant. "Complicity: How Connecticut Chained Itself to Slavery." *Northeast Magazine.* Hartford, CT: Hartford Courant, 2002.

Fales, Edward, Jr., ed. *Arsenal of the Revolution: The First History of the "Fourteenth Colony."* Lakeville, CT: Lakeville Journal and the News, 1976.

Geiling, Natash. "The Worst Shark Attack in History." *Smithsonian Magazine.* August 8, 2013.

Giguere, Judith. "The Witch of Fall Mountain." http://www.plymouthct.us/index.cfm?fuseaction=content.faq&faqTypeID=40019 (accessed December 19, 2015).

Goodenough, Arthur. *The Clergy of Litchfield County.* Winchester, CT: Litchfield University Club, 1990.

Goodheart, Lawrence B. *The Solemn Sentence of Death: Capital Punishment in Connecticut.* Amherst: University of Massachusetts Press, 2011.

Grant, Charles S. *Democracy in the Connecticut Frontier Town of Kent.* New York: AMS Press, 1979.

Grant, Ellsworth S. *The Miracle of Connecticut.* Hartford: Connecticut Historical Society, 1992.

Hall, Charles Swain. *Benjamin Tallmadge: Revolutionary Soldier and American Businessman.* New York: Columbia University Press, 1943.

History of Litchfield County, Connecticut, with Illustrations and Biographical Sketches of its Prominent Men and Pioneers. Philadelphia: J.W. Lewis & Company, 1881.

Hoyt, Edwin P. *The Damnedest Yankees: Ethan Allen and his Clan.* Brattleboro, VT: Stephen Greene Press, 1976.

Jellison, Charles A. *Ethan Allen: Frontier Rebel.* Syracuse, NY: Syracuse University Press, 1969.

Kilbourn, Dwight. *The Bench and Bar of Litchfield County, Connecticut, 1709–1909.* Litchfield, CT: Privately Published, 1909.

Kilbourne, Payne Kenyon. *Sketches and Chronicles of the Town of Litchfield, Connecticut.* Hartford, CT: Case, Lockwood & Company, 1859.

Mars, James. *Life of James Mars, A Slave Bought and Sold in Connecticut. Written by Himself.* Hartford: Case, Lockwood and Company, 1864.

Menschel, David. "Abolition Without Deliverance: The Law of Connecticut Slavery, 1784–1848." *Yale Law Journal* 111, no. 1 (2001).

One Hundred Years: History of Morris, Connecticut, 1859–1959. N.p.: Morris Centennial Committee, 1959.

Orcutt, Samuel. *History of the Towns of New Milford and Bridgewater, Connecticut, 1703–1882.* Hartford, CT: Case, Lockwood and Company, 1882.

———. *History of Torrington, Connecticut.* Albany, NY: J. Munsell, 1878.

Parker, Wyman. *Connecticut's Colonial and Continental Money.* Hartford: American Revolution Bicentennial Commission of Connecticut, 1976.

Payne, Charles Thomas. *Litchfield and Morris Inscriptions: A Record of Inscriptions Upon the Tombstones of Litchfield and Morris, CT.* Litchfield, CT: Dwight C. Kilbourn, 1905.

Philbrick, Nathaniel. *Sea of Glory: America's Voyage of Discovery: The U.S. Exploring Expedition, 1838–1842.* New York: Viking Press, 2003.

Philips, David E. *Legendary Connecticut: Traditional Tales from the Nutmeg State.* Hartford, CT: Spoonwood Press, 1984.

Randall, Willard Sterne. *Ethan Allen: His Life and Times.* New York: W.W. Norton, 2011.

Richards, Josephine Ellis, ed. *Honor Roll of the Litchfield County Revolutionary Soldiers*. Litchfield, CT: Mary Floyd Tallmadge Chapter, Daughters of the American Revolution, 1912.

Rose, Alexander. *Washington's Spies*. New York: Bantam, 2014.

Sedgwick, Charles F. *General History of the Town of Sharon from its First Settlement*. Amenia, NY: Charles Walsh, 1877.

Spooner, Clifford C. "The Story of Molly Fisher and the Molly Fisher Rock." 1930. Reprinted from *Kent Tales* on www.schaghticoke.net/coltsfoot/skyweb/skywebspooner.html (accessed October 9, 2015).

Stanton, Doug. *In Harm's Way: The Sinking of the USS* Indianapolis *and the Extraordinary Story of its Survivors*. New York: Henry Holt and Company, 2001.

Sterry, Iveagh Hunt. *They Found a Way: Connecticut's Restless People*. Brattleboro, VT: Stephen Daye Press, 1938.

Strong, Barbara Nolen. *The Morris Academy: Pioneer in Coeducation*. Morris, CT: Morris Bicentennial Committee, 1976.

Strother, Horatio. *The Underground Railroad in Connecticut*. Middletown, CT: Wesleyan University Press, 1962.

Tarnoff, Ben. *Moneymakers: The Wicked Lives and Surprising Adventures of Three Notorious Counterfeiters*. New York: Penguin Press, 2011.

Taylor, John M. *The Witchcraft Delusion in Colonial Connecticut, 1647–1697*. Stratford, CT: J. Edmund Edwards, 1969.

Tomlinson, R.G. *Witchcraft Prosecution: Chasing the Devil in Connecticut*. Rockland, ME: Picton Press, 2012.

"The United States Exploring Expedition." Smithsonian Libraries. http://www.sil.si.edu/digitalcollections/usexex/ (accessed October 9, 2015).

Vermilyea, Peter C. *Hidden History of Litchfield County*. Charleston, SC: The History Press, 2014.

Works Consulted

Warshauer, Matthew. *Connecticut in the American Civil War: Slavery, Sacrifice and Survival*. Middletown, CT: Wesleyan University Press, 2012.

Welch, Richard F. *General Washington's Commando: Benjamin Tallmadge in the Revolutionary War*. Jefferson, NC: McFarland, 2014.

White, Alain C. *The History of the Town of Litchfield, Connecticut, 1720–1920*. Litchfield, CT: Litchfield Historical Society, 1920.

Woodruff, George C. *History of the Town of Litchfield, Connecticut*. Litchfield, CT: C. Adams, 1845.

"The Worst Naval Disaster in US History." www.ussindianapolis.org (accessed October 9, 2015).

Yates, Neil E. *Two Roads to Community: The First 150 Years of Northwest Community Bank*. Winsted, CT: Northwest Community Bank, 2010.

ABOUT THE AUTHOR

*P*eter C. Vermilyea teaches history at Housatonic Valley Regional High School in Falls Village, Connecticut, and at Western Connecticut State University. A graduate of Gettysburg College, he is the director of the student scholarship program at his alma mater's Civil War Institute. Vermilyea is the author or editor of four books, including *Hidden History of Litchfield County* (The History Press, 2014), which received the 2015 CultureMax Award, and more than a dozen articles, mostly on Civil War history, and maintains the Hidden in Plain Sight blog, www.hiddeninplainsightblog.com. He lives in Litchfield, Connecticut, with his wife and two sons.

Visit us at
www.historypress.net
....
This title is also available as an e-book